VISUALIZATION

VISUALIZATION:

Directing the Movies of Your Mind

ADELAIDE BRY

with **MARJORIE BAIR**

PERENNIAL LIBRARY

Harper & Row, Publishers
New York, Cambridge, Philadelphia, San Francisco
London, Mexico City, São Paulo, Singapore, Sydney

Portions of this work originally appeared in *New Woman.*

Grateful acknowledgment is made for permission to reprint the following:

"Life is Like a Motion Picture" by Hime Ilili. Copyright, 1976, Ilili Music, Inc. B.M.

Exercises on pages 36, 100, 101, and 158 reprinted by permission of Win Wenger.

Excerpt on page 11 from *The Psychology of Consciousness* by Robert Ornstein. Copyright © 1972 by Harcourt Brace Jovanovich, Inc. Reprinted by permission of Harcourt Brace Jovanovich, Inc.

Drawings on pages 92 and 93 courtesy of Dr. Jeanne Achterberg.

First BARNES AND NOBLE BOOKS edition published 1979.

ISBN: 0–06–464033–7

88 89 90   20 19 18 17 16 15 14 13

LOVE TO MY FATHER

Acknowledgments

I had a superb personal odyssey as I circled the country to meet with men and women who are using pictures-in-the-mind in a variety of ways.

As I began to think of all the people involved in this book, I had no idea the list would be as long as it is. I thank each one of you for your unique contribution.

A very special thanks to Jerry Jampolsky.

Michael Bookbinder, Dr. Peter Brill, Barbara Bry, Jack Canfield, Sally Carr, Werner Erhard, Dr. James Fadiman, Dr. Edward Frost, Anita Halpert, Dr. Herbert Hamsher, Hime, Peggy Huddleston, Ilili, Michael Karp, Stanley Krippner, Dr. Robert Leichtman, Mimi Lupin, Dr. O. W. Markley, Robert McKim, Michael Murphy, Dr. Irving Oyle, John Page, Dr. Kenneth Pelletier, David Rich, John Robinson, David Rosen, Dr. Marty Rossman, Stuart Scheingarten, Judi Skutch, Dr. George Solomon, Patricia Sun, Robert Toporek, Hugh Townley, Win Wenger, Catherine West, Dr. Lance Wright, and Al Zuckerman.

Contents

LIFE IS LIKE A MOTION PICTURE

Life is like a motion picture
on a great big screen.
And you are the director
directing all your scenes.
You write the script,
you cast it too.
And in the leading role
The star of your film is—
YOU!

Life is like a motion picture,
a technicolor dream,
and through your eyes the camera
is projecting scene on scene.
The plot unfolds both night and day.
Sometimes you're lost,
then you find your way.

So follow your star.
The star you are
in the great big movie of your mind.

—HIME ILILI

Preface

If there is a single moment in writing this book that stands out above the others, it happened—appropriately—during a movie-of-the-mind.

I was lying on the thick beige rug in my living room, my eyes closed, and in a state of marvelous relaxation. Stretched out on one side of me was my co-author, Marjorie Bair. On the other side, sitting cross-legged and looking content with his own inner experience, was Win Wenger, friend and creator of Psychegenics who had made a special trip to Philadelphia to be with us. (Not so long ago I would have thought lying on the floor this way was ridiculous, but now I fully accepted this part of me. It was symbolic of all the other things I had once thought ludicrous—and which had since become invaluable in my life.)

For the umpteenth time, but, paradoxically, for the first time using movies-of-the-mind, I asked the question that had yet to find an answer through months of travel, research, and intense inner exploration:

How can we present the incredible truth about inner movies in a way that will touch people deeply, help them move closer to wholeness and happiness, open them to this extraordinarily meaningful process, and allow us to experience the success that would naturally follow?

My images that afternoon were a delight—sometimes funny, sometimes outrageous, always fascinating. But the answer evaded me. I saw the completed book displayed in bookstores. I even saw my editor and publisher looking pleased with it.

Then, again, I asked the question. And the answer came this time. It came—in the form of a picture and words—with the clarity, conviction and authority that signaled that I had touched the truth.

A lovely golden child suddenly appeared in the space before me. Smiling, with its arms outstretched, it had an aura both of pure innocence and profound wisdom. It also conveyed a very powerful feeling of love, which I found myself deeply moved by. Then it delivered its message—and was gone. The words that lingered on were the only sign that it had been there.

"Speak to the golden child in each and every one."

The message was almost embarrassingly simple, as the truth often is, but I knew immediately that it was the key that had evaded me. The image of the golden child symbolized the *beautiful, loving, knowing,* and *spontaneous* being that you and I each are, even if most of us don't yet fully know it. It was that part of you that I would speak to and nurture on these pages.

A marvelous belly laugh swept through me as I explored this image. Marjorie, alongside me, had followed my movie through my narration and was herself waiting for an answer to the question. In her own movie she had discovered a billboard and, in the course of our simultaneous visualization, had tested a number of different images and phrases on it. But none had felt quite right. When she heard what had come to me, she knew instantly that it was what she was waiting for. She projected the image of a beautiful golden child on her billboard and she, too, began to laugh.

It was our sense of the absurd that triggered our hilarity that May afternoon on my living-room floor.

Just a few yards away, in my office, were reams of notes and huge piles of papers, tracts, and both scholarly and popular books related to the subject of visualization. I had criss-crossed the country several times to meet the people who were doing pioneer work in this area and had read everything I could find on the subject. And I had immersed myself deeply in the process itself, so that no aspect of my life had not been touched and strengthened by it.

Now, ironically, I found that the key to this book was not through all that data I had so diligently accumulated. Although the research was essential, far more important for what we sought to do was to create a link between our hearts and yours—between the best in us and the best in you.

And so I begin this book by inviting you to think of yourself as a lovely golden child—very beautiful, very wise, and very loving. It is that part of you that you will discover and get to know here.

ADELAIDE BRY

Bala Cynwyd, Pa.
1978

VISUALIZATION

1

How Directing the Movies of Your Mind Will Help You in Your Life

Mere mental activity does not bring a change of consciousness; it only brings a change of mind.

—Sri Aurobindo

A dear friend of mine telephoned me a few months ago in a state of total despair.

"I simply can't get him out of my mind," Jane told me through her sobs. "I need help. Something . . . anything . . . to get me through this."

The "him" she was speaking about was the man she had lived with for the past ten years. They had been lovers and friends, but their increasing difficulty in communicating with each other had placed a heavy strain on their relationship. In a moment of rage, Jane demanded that he leave the house they had shared for so long. But in the days that followed, *reason* again took precedence over feelings and she had a change of *mind*. She asked him to change his mind as well, but he was hurt and told her that he *believed* that a reconciliation was impossible.

Since then, Jane had made her life miserable. Plagued with guilt, convinced that she had made a dreadful mistake, certain she still loved him—these *thoughts* which ran nonstop through her mind had paralyzed her. As long as she *believed* that the only solution lay in her lover's return, she remained stuck and unhappy.

My first impulse, as a therapist, was to present her with other *thoughts* and *reasonings* and *beliefs* directed to her *mind* in an effort to change it. But I knew that ultimately these wouldn't be any more helpful than her own self-defeating mental acrobatics. Jane needed to go beyond words and thoughts to an entirely different experience of the problem.

Coincidentally, I had just returned from California where I had met a number of physicians and psychiatrists who were using *movies-of-the-mind* in their medical and psychotherapy practice, and I was deeply impressed with the results they were getting. I thought that a technique used by Dr. Irving Oyle, in particular, would be especially relevant here. I gave Jane a quick description of what it was all about, and she arrived minutes later ready for her very first movie-of-the-mind.

I instructed her first to relax. As you will soon discover, becoming deeply relaxed is the essential first step in directing your own movies-of-the-mind. Then, with her eyes closed, I suggested that she imagine a beautiful calm lake on a warm summer's day. I suggested that she see the trees surrounding the lake and then feel in her body a sense of serenity and peace.

After these pictures were clear, I told her to let an animal, any animal, come up to her as she sat on the shore of that lake. When it did, I suggested that she engage it in conversation. "Share your problem with the animal. It's there to help you," I assured her, "and wants to know how. When you feel comfortable with that animal, ask it how it feels about your decision to end your relationship."

At first Jane thought my suggestions absurd, but then she agreed to follow them. She became quiet and turned her attention to her inner movie screen. There she stayed for several minutes until, with a telling giggle, she signaled that she had found what she had come for.

She began her "trip" reluctantly, she told me, thinking the instructions "dumb"; later she realized that some of her reluctance had to do with not fully wanting to face the truth. As she gradually gave over to the experience the pictures became clear and unavoidably compelling.

Jane saw herself at the edge of the lake in Maine where she had spent summers as a child. Suddenly and incongruously a huge orangutan emerged from the woods and stood in front of her. From the moment it appeared, she found that she knew all sorts of things about it. She knew, for example, that it was male. And she knew beyond any doubt that he had something important to tell her.

The two of them sat down together and began to talk. When she asked him about her relationship, he smiled and told her very exactly what he thought about it. First, he said, she knew that she had made the exactly right decision for herself at this point in her life. "You very much want to grow in another direction in your life," he explained, "but you're afraid to do that. One way you avoid it is by taking refuge in the idea that you need to stay in the relationship." He went on to say that she might have become seriously ill had the relationship continued, as it was taking a heavy toll on her emotionally. "You are going through a difficult time of separation," he told her, "but you need it to release you to flow in a different direction now. That's what's best for you."

Jane was awed by what had happened to her. "When I heard the orangutan's words, I knew instantly that it was the absolute and utter truth," she told me. She realized that she hadn't wanted to know it and had preferred, instead, to feel guilty and miserable and thus mired in a situation that she knew was wrong for her. All the thinking she had done about it had only served to hide this realization from herself.

The Orangutan . . . and You

Just as Jane had an image of an orangutan available to her at the flick of her inner camera's switch, so do you have images within you that may be strange or funny or beautiful but which you're not aware of. These images can help you in innumerable ways. As it did through Jane's orangutan, an image can bypass the thoughts that run through your mind to give you an entirely new dimension on your life.

"But," you may be saying to yourself, *"I* can't do *that."* And if that's not the protest that comes to mind, how about: "But it sounds ridiculous" or "I don't believe it"? There might be some others as well.

Let me begin by assuring you unequivocally that you *can* create movies in your mind. Not only do you already know how to do this—to perfection—but you do it all the time. You do it every time you remember something. You do it every time you daydream. You do it every time you think of someone. And, let me add, you do it without being aware of doing it in a thousand different situations every day.

I suggest that you try it right now. Lift your eyes from this book and look at the nearest lamp on the nearest table. Examine it in detail. Note its color, texture and shape. Now notice the way the light casts shadows. Take in everything you see about the lamp.

When you have noted everything there is to note about the lamp from where you're sitting, close your eyes and picture in your mind's eye the lamp you have just seen, If you can do that, you can direct the movies of your mind. What you've just experienced *is* a movie of your mind.

The way you may have seen this lamp on your inner screen varies from person to person. Some see their pictures in technicolor, others in black and white. Some see their pictures in very clear detail; for others the images are fuzzy or in shadow or they simply have a "sense" of the object on their inner screen. As long as what you experience is other than words, we'll call it a picture. Like anything else in life, practice makes perfect. A fuzzy lamp today . . . a magnificent multicolored tableau tomorrow!

Here's another exercise, a different kind of remembering that you also can experience on your inner movie screen.

Close your eyes and see with your inner eye the kitchen of your home. Note its arrangement. Observe the appliances, the cabinets, the kitchen table, and chairs. Then see if there are any cracks in the ceiling, and notice the condition of the floor and walls. You can look for anything else that you're curious about as well.

As with the previous exercise, you might get an exact replica of the real thing, a vague impression, or something in-between. *If you get anything, then be assured that you can direct the movies of your mind.*

These preliminary "scripts" just give you a hint of what's to come. As you experience your inner pictures in more significant ways, and read the stories of people like you who use their movies with amazing results, whatever skepticism you still may have will quickly fade.

However new the notion may seem to you now, creating movies-of-the-mind is a human skill that each and every one of us possesses. This book merely shows you how to do it the best and most rewarding way for your particular self.

Why Movies-of-the-Mind Instead of Words

One of the things unique to modern Western culture is that almost all our experience is understood through the logical, linear, analytical thinking process. The main way we communicate this kind of thinking—to ourselves and to others—is through words. Words have become our primary way of knowing, of being with each other, and of understanding the world around us.

Somewhere along the way most of us have forgotten that we have another side. As we founder in a sea of rationality, immersed in our thoughts and words, we get further and further away from our intuitive, creative selves. In doing this, we also move further away from the direct experience of ourselves as the cause, or "creator," of our lives.

One of the things that happens when we are continually cut off from our intuition is that our minds become trapped in a circle of thoughts and ideas learned a long time ago. Yesterday's beliefs can't solve today's problems. Nor do they bring much light to tomorrow's possibilities.

Another thing that happens is that we begin to confuse the words and thoughts *about* our experiences with the experiences themselves. In doing this we deprive ourselves of fully knowing that we are the source of the patterns and events of our lives. Through our movies-of-the-mind, however, we can create a state of awareness in which we are *not thinking about,* or *figuring out,* or *analyzing* our experiences, *but actually experiencing them directly.* To paraphrase Werner Erhard, creator of the est training, this allows us to rediscover ourselves as the *cause,* rather than being *at the effect,* of the quality of our lives—and thus win out over life.

Having mastered a great many ideas and thoughts—ranging from long division in the fifth grade to the theories of Freud and Jung much later in life—I have only recently discovered that they have little relevance to who I am and will become, how I am in the world, and what happens in my life.

In contrast, since I have begun using the movies of *my* mind—watching them, enjoying them, sometimes being frightened by them, always letting them be what they want to be—I have found a new meaning, a new direction, and a new sense of control in my life. Unlike the intellect, from which our thoughts and words come and whose resources are inevitably limited, I have found that inner movies are a tool of unlimited richness that never goes dull, never gets repetitious, and always brings a fresh perspective to life.

Directing an inner movie is a special way of using your imagination which, as you will discover later in this book, can change what is going on in your body as much as it can influence what happens in your day-to-day living. As doctors and others now know from the science of biofeedback, the rate of our heartbeat and other body functions can be altered by changing what we're feeling and thinking. And as students of the mind are rediscovering from the writings of artists and scientists throughout history, solutions to seemingly insoluble problems can be found by tuning in to our inner images.

The more you and I experience movies-of-the-mind, the more we will be able to take hold of our lives and control them in a new way. Our inner experience is so directly connected to our outer experience, in fact, that what we can project onto our inner movie screens, we can experience in real life.

How can this affect our moment-to-moment living?

People who use movies-of-the-mind often find themselves refusing painkillers for their headaches, rejections from their lovers, and martyrdom from their mothers, among other things. They find, instead, more effective ways to deal with their health, relationships, and interactions.

If there are ghosts in your past, if you have a pervasive sense of inadequacy, unresolved or uncomfortable feelings that upset you—those experiences which permeate our thoughts and yet are so hard to verbalize can be dealt with in an entirely new way, through movies-of-the-mind. By contacting and exploring them at a deeper level than you have previously reached, it becomes possible also to feel less conflicted, more serene, and more peaceful than ever before.

Consider that the lifetime you'll spend here on earth can be entirely different from your dreary expectations of it. Instead of a time of quiet desperation, it can be a time of infinite and joyous possibility.

These are not empty promises. Happily, they are totally possible. Farther on in these pages, you will learn how to use movies-of-the-mind for very specific situations. For now, what's most important is that you begin to consider that beyond the steady stream of words and thoughts that consume you is a vast area of incredible richness that most of us never get to know.

The people I encounter who are most whole, most alive, and most fulfilled are not those who have mastered only the intellectual world of facts and logic. Rather, they are those who have looked inside themselves seeking to know themselves.

How you, too, can discover the mysteries within you—and in doing so expand every dimension of your life—is what I hope to help you do here. Through my own experiences, through the experiences of friends, acquaintances, and patients, through the research being done in a variety of disciplines, the potential in this new area of human exploration will unfold for you. As it does, so also will you find yourself unfolding.

2

Say Hello to the Part of Your Mind You've Been Ignoring

> The words or the language as they are written and spoken do not seem to play any role in my mechanism of thought.
>
> —Albert Einstein

Beginning at the beginning, let me tell you about movies-of-the-mind. What they are. Where they come from. What you need in order to "do" them. And why I think they're the most important new tool at our service to expand and enrich our lives.

Movies-of-the-mind—which I also refer to as visualization, inner pictures, images, and more generally, the inner experience—have actually been known and explored since the beginning of time. Like other "irrational" pursuits which we're now taking a fresh look at (dreams, astrology, meditation, etc.), their use in recent times had for the most part been narrowed to mystics and shamans. Today, updated variations of visualization are being used by a growing variety of people: physicians, psychotherapists, athletes, teachers, dieters, artists, business people, and lovers—to name just a few.

It was the beginning of our conquest of *outer* space a decade ago that first turned our attention back to *inner* space. In search of a "last frontier," we looked to that most neglected of subjects: the human mind. We had become very sophisticated about the world around us but actually knew very little about the world within us.

And so we began exploring this part of ourselves with a fresh curiosity and respect. We approached it from basically two points of view. One grew out of the "human potential" movement, which sought to go beyond what we could know with the senses and conscious mind; this was spearheaded by psychologists and became known as the "consciousness" movement. The other emerged from the scientific community and focused on brain research; in its vanguard were physicians and biologists.

One of the most important things we discovered from all this was that the mind was far more complicated and resourceful than we had ever imagined.

Thinking and Knowing: The Difference

We learned that the brain is divided into two distinct parts, each with every different functions and areas of influence. The left side of the brain is basically concerned with the logical and verbal. It thinks. The right side of the brain is related to the intuitive and creative. It knows. The following will help you understand the difference.

Imagine a long freight train moving down a railroad track as seen by two people from very different vantage points.

One person is standing on the ground, about three feet from the track, and is looking directly ahead of him at the train as it passes. Out of the corners of his eyes he can glimpse that part of the train that has already passed as well as that part which will pass momentarily. Mostly what he sees is what is passing right in front of him from moment to moment—first the engine, then the first car, then the second car and on and on, until finally the caboose has come and gone. This is the way the left, or logical, side of the brain functions.

Imagine, now, another person watching that same train at the same time. This person is high up in the air, perhaps in a balloon. From her vantage point above the train she perceives it entirely differently from the person on the ground. Instead of seeing it one car at a time, she sees it all at once. This intuitive, all-at-once, holistic view is the way the right side of the brain functions.

To give you a better idea of the differences between these two sides of your brain, here is a list borrowed from Robert E. Ornstein:*

The Left Side	**The Right Side**
Connected to the right side of the body, and the right side of each eye's vision.	Connected to the left side of the body, and the left side of each eye's vision.
Deals with inputs one at a time.	Demands ready integration of many inputs at once.
Processes information in a linear manner. Has a lineal and sequential mode of operation.	Processes information more diffusely. Has a nonlineal and simultaneous mode of operation.
Deals with time. Responsible for the faculty of verbal expression, or language.	Deals with space. Responsible for gestures, facial and body movements (or "body language"), tone of voice, etc.
Responsible for verbal and mathematical functions.	Responsible for spatial and relational functions; awareness of our bodies; for sports and dancing; our orientation in space; recognition of faces; artistic endeavor; musical ability and recognition of pitch.

(cont'd)

* Robert E. Ornstein, *The Psychology of Consciousness.* (New York: Harcourt Brace Jovanovich, 1972).

(cont'd)

The Left Side	The Right Side
Specializes in memory and recognition of words or numbers.	Specializes in memory and recognition of objects, persons, and places, music, etc.
Normally tends to specialize in logic and analytical reasoning or thinking.	Normally tends to specialize in intuition and holistic perception or thinking.
The seat of reason.	The seat of passion and of dreams.
The crucial side of the brain for wordsmiths, mathematicians, and scientists.	The crucial side of the brain for artists, crafts people, musicians.

It is the right side of our brains that we have neglected, beginning as children when we were encouraged to focus on the three R's, later as teen-agers when we were admonished to stop daydreaming, still later as young adults when everything that seemed important to us required developing our left-brain talents. But while we strengthened and nurtured our intellects, we weakened and all but forgot about the intuitive and spontaneous side of ourselves. Although *it* continued to function, *we* became insensitive to it. Fortunately, some people never lost touch with this part of themselves; among them are those who give us the art and poetry that embellish our lives.

Without the full use of our "right-brains," we are at best using only half of our potential. Like those who have favored one foot over another, we have wound up limping and lopsided. But that part of us is always accessible, if only we choose to reach inward to it. Once we have rediscovered it, we can then allow it to work cooperatively with the more highly developed "left-brain." In that way we can finally begin to experience the full potential of our minds.

An example of how these two functions work together, in shifting but complementary rhythms, is illustrated by the way this book evolved. While my left-brain directed, accumulated, and processed the necessary research, my right-brain contributed the inspirations, connections, and insights that make it more than the sum of that research. Although I didn't give exactly equal time to right- and left-brain activity, at least not consciously, I did come close. Some of my most productive moments were experienced while I lay in bed at night, imagining myself on my favorite Caribbean beach.

Another example comes from that champion of the intellect Albert Einstein, who said emphatically that his creative brainstorms did not come from his "mind," but from another place entirely. "The words or the language, as they are written and spoken, do not seem to play any role in my mechanism of thought," he once wrote. "The . . . entities which seem to serve as elements in thought are . . . more-or-less-clear *images* [my italics] which can be 'voluntarily' reproduced and combined."*

Although this book shows you how to use your intuitive mind, I want to make clear that it should not be at the expense of the logical, rational mind. What we need to do is to awaken that which is dormant in us, allow it to emerge, and then let it join its more conspicuous partner in a more equal relationship. Both are beautiful.

Movies-of-the-mind are, of course, a right-brain experience. They bypass the limitations of the cognitive, rational, analytical, linear thinking mind and tap the limitless source from which our emotions, intuitions, creativity, and imagination flow. This is the place, also, in which everything we've ever known can be rediscovered.

As we begin to observe our inner movies, we find that the experience is totally unlike what happens to us when we "think."

* From Albert Einstein's "Letter to Jacques Hadamard," quoted in *The Creative Process,* ed. Brewster Ghiselin (New York: New American Library, 1952).

Through visualization, we can look at past, present, and future in the same way, a few pages back, we looked at the train from a perch high above it—with a sense of how the train is all of a piece. At a practical level, visualization has an uncanny ability to improve the quality of our lives. It does this through its power to heal the body and spirit, to reconstruct the past, and to reveal our hidden truths. This inner experience can also take us way beyond the practical. The most dramatic visualizations touch the deepest part of ourselves—our essence, or core—and allow us to experience connections beyond ourselves, what some describe as cosmic consciousness.

The One Thing You Need to Visualize

This is not magic I am writing about. As you have discovered, you already have all the sensitivity and skill you need to direct the movies of your mind. The one thing you need in addition to these inborn qualities is your willingness.

The willingness I speak of here is a willingness to experience yourself fully. It is a willingness to feel your full aliveness, to be the very best that you can be, to realize your unique and beautiful potential. It is a willingness, above all, to be happy. Strange as that may seem, a desire to be happy may be the single most important prerequisite for getting what you want out of life. And possibly the most difficult to experience without conflict.

Although most of us could make a strong case for proving that we live our lives in pursuit of happiness, actually a lot of our energy goes into *sabotaging* our happiness. We do it in a million small and large ways. We do it often and in some cases continually. We do it for dozens of reasons, but the most essential one is our unconscious belief that we're not entitled to happiness. We see life as something to be endured—with, if we're lucky, good times now and then.

Feeling entitled to happiness is certainly not something most of us grew up with. We were told that we either had to work harder than we wanted to in order to earn happiness, or better still, not expect it at all. The idea of concentrating on ways to make ourselves happy was—and to some extent still is— considered morally unacceptable. This belief ignores the truth that denying one's own best interests also denies the needs of those we care about. Conversely, the healthier, more radiant, more fulfilled, and happier we are, the more we are able to share these qualities with others.

As some of you know through my book, *est: 60 Hours That Transform Your Life,* I am a graduate of the est training created by Werner Erhard. Since that experience a few years ago, I have continued to expand my joy in life—deepening existing friendships, creating warm and wonderful new ones, and finding increasing satisfaction in my work and play. But as I now look back, the single, most transforming experience I had was that of Werner Erhard himself.

In Werner I discovered living proof that the more we are, the more we have to give. His aliveness and the love he radiates touch and inspire almost all who come in contact with him. The trainers who work with him have these same qualities, with similar wonderful effects. It was through my contact with these very special people that I first realized that each and every one of us can have this same feeling of aliveness and well-being. We carry it with us all the time, but it is buried underneath all the things we do to deny and ignore it. In using our right-brain powers (which, incidentally, are an important focus of the est training), we can begin to unload the debris that keeps us only half alive.

This is a process that takes time and patience, but I see now that life itself is a continuing process. As much as we might want instant aliveness, our prime responsibility to ourselves is to continue to grow and expand one step at a time, strengthening our capacity for love and happiness, moving ever closer to a state of harmony within ourselves and with others.

I also see now that our most cherished tool for growth and learning—our thinking, or left, brain—has been overdeveloped at the expense of the equally important intuitional and feeling right-brain.

As a result, we have become isolated, alienated beings identified with our heads and living uneasily in our bodies and our feelings. We have come to see our lives as meaningless and beyond our control, and so we settle for *coping with* or *curing* our dissatisfactions, problems, neuroses, and ailments.

I see now that it can be otherwise.

When I began writing this book I considered visualization an effective technique to be added to a repertoire of self-help techniques. But I discovered, as I began meeting with people working in this infant field, that at the time my experience of visualization was just a tiny aspect of something far bigger.

In Tiburon, California, I met a physician who was liberating children from their learning problems by having them picture taking out their brains, washing them, and then returning them freshly bathed.

In San Francisco I talked with a psychologist who had co-founded a holistic medical center in which visualization was being used as one of several approaches to healing based on the power of the mind. His patients had become fully convinced that they were in control of both their illnesses and their paths back to health.

Elsewhere I met the head of a multi-million-dollar shipping company who was using visualization for himself and his staff to expand his business.

I met a woman who had lost thirty-five pounds, the coach of an Olympic team who had dramatically improved his team's performance, and people who had gotten remission from cancer—all by their directing the movies of their minds.

The one thing they and the others I was to speak with had in common was that none of them *blamed* fate or bad luck or their parents or their doctors or anyone else for their circumstances. Regardless of their philosophical, religious, or psychological orientation, they all were assuming responsibility for their health and illness, their success and failure, their happiness and misery.

This is in dramatic contrast to what I had encountered as a therapist. Most of the people who had come to me arrived with an overwhelming sense of inadequacy and despair. They regarded themselves as "victims" of everything from their parents to their financial situation to their illnesses. Whatever they had *believed* about themselves is what they had *become*. In varying degrees, they had been trying to change the problem situations in their lives. But nowhere along the way had they channeled their *real power,* the power of their intuitive resources to transform their destructive, life-denying impulses.

In my own personal odyssey, I keep finding new ways to help both myself and those with whom I work. As I venture more deeply into myself I keep discovering more and more of the treasures that lie within. And I find there is no end to them. I feel more "connected" than I ever imagined possible. And I now begin to see the interconnectedness of everything in the universe, including you and me.

3

The What and Why of Creating Movies of the Mind

> Space flights are merely an escape, a fleeing away from oneself, because it is easier to go to Mars or to the moon than it is to penetrate one's own being.
>
> —Carl Jung

Borrowing from modern technology for an analogy, a movie-of-the-mind is a special kind of "home movie" in which you are screenwriter, producer, director, star, and cameraperson. This home movie can go anywhere in time and space and can unreel any type of material you want to view. It comes to you uncensored, direct from the recesses of your mind, and is unfailingly accurate, interesting, and meaningful.

More specifically, movies-of-the-mind is:

• A method of developing inner awareness and control of the body's autonomic functions.

• A way to bring to consciousness what you really feel and to understand the meaning of the things that occur in your life.

• A way to get in touch with your imaginative powers.

• A source of information much vaster than words.

• A channel, for many, to personal and universal truth.

• And, most important, it is an act of conscious and deliberate creating.

Where Has It Been All My Life?

Dormant.

Hidden behind the incessant thoughts and words which race through our minds and preoccupy us, and of which we're only vaguely aware.

Rejected and forgotten during our (Western society's) long love affair with the rational, logical, and objective.

Stashed away because some aspects of it may have been— or continue to be—frightening to us.

Ignored because it seems irrelevant, untrustworthy, weird, and until the last few years, definitely unfashionable.

Carl Jung wrote shortly before his death: "Space flights are merely an escape, a fleeing away from oneself, because it is easier to go to Mars or to the moon than it is to penetrate one's own being."

In many ways it appears that primitive and myth-making man had a much greater sense of himself than we do today. Although he wasn't sufficiently developed to have invented an airplane or discovered DNA, he made better use of the mind power he did have, using the word *mind* in its broadest sense. He was in touch with his inner processes, and the unseen forces within and beyond himself with which he interacted. And he regarded as inseparable his body, mind, and spirit.

The more civilized we have become, the more sophisticated our development in the areas of science, medicine, and mathematics, the more we dissociate ourselves from the real source of our creativity. It is ironic, because many of the geniuses of recent centuries—Einstein, Mozart, Darwin, Bertrand Russell, Tchaikovsky, to name a few—have acknowledged that their most creative ideas emerged as spontaneous, *non-thinking* inspirations.

Whether our attachment to rationality, science, and technology has come about in response to our fear of exploring our "inner being," or simply because the rewards of rationality have been more seductive than those of the contemplative life, is an intriguing issue for speculation. The fact remains that although we have chosen to cut ourselves off from our inner movies, each and every one of us has them.

Our movies began the day we were born (and maybe earlier) and we add footage to them every moment of every day, with every conscious and unconscious thought and act.

These inner movies contain all our experiences, including all those we don't think it possible to remember: the feelings of cold, warmth, wet, and hunger we had as infants; the parental "no's" that so deeply influenced us; our own past and present "no's" (as well as "yeses") to life; and, within all these unconscious images, the seeds of future experiences.

Since visualization is a common human ability, these movies are available to us for screening any time we choose to look at them.

I would like to repeat here that this book is not at all a case against intellectual development. Our thinking mind has served our society—and certainly me, personally—very well. But in viewing the mind as little more than the source of our thoughts, we betray that part of us that gives meaning and purpose to what we do. We betray, also, our individual and collective potential for growth and expansion.

Some Thoughts About Thinking

Since we are talking a lot about thinking and *not* thinking here, you should have some idea of what it is we do when we think.

Most of our thinking is a circular series of odds and ends that we're only vaguely aware of. Our thoughts have to do with the little gnawing details of our lives—what we will and won't do, did and didn't do, should and shouldn't do—and all the self-judgments with them. They nag and gossip and worry in endless repetition. Most of all, they continually evaluate as good, bad, or indifferent everyone we interact with and everything that happens to us.

Our thoughts do these things in no particular order and without any sense of priority. And so, in a thirty-second span of thinking you might be reminded to buy milk, note that the star of last night's TV show looked terrible, worry about the balance in your checking account, and chastise yourself for saying something dumb to the mailman. You can have these sorts of thoughts either in the midst of *deliberately* thinking about an important issue in your life or when you're pretty sure you're not thinking at all.

This kind of thinking is not only unproductive, but by filling up our minds, it also keeps us from knowing what *else* is going on inside us. Some of the things we don't notice because of the continual mental chit-chat are our feelings and intuitions. But trying to stop our thoughts to allow these other things to come to mind isn't easy.

Try it. For a minute or so close your eyes and stop thinking. While you're doing this, try to be fully aware of what's happening inside you. The object is to make and keep your mind totally blank for this brief span of time. If any thoughts pop into the blankness, just look at them and let them move on.

Unless you're a seasoned meditator, or went to sleep, you undoubtedly found it practically impossible to stop your thoughts. You did, however, get a terrific first-hand look at how you think. If you were hoping to find gems of wisdom and instead found a stream of trivia, be reassured that even the most brilliant among us are often preoccupied with drivel.

What most of us believe is "thinking" is actually a combination of both our thinking and intuitive processes. When you decide to "figure it out," what happens is that the part of you that "figures" takes what it already knows and rearranges it over and over again, stopping only when the solution suddenly "just comes" to you. You assumed that what you got was the product of "weighing all the possibilities" and "making up your mind." What you ultimately got actually came from another process entirely. It was the right-brain at work, and the answer came in a characteristically right-brain way—as a sudden "aha!" You then immediately put your intellect to work by checking out your right-brain insight with your left-brain logic.

What you will learn to do through movies-of-the-mind is to think in a way that makes optimum use of this natural process. You'll discover how and when to use your right-brain. Just as important, you'll also learn how and when *not* to use your left-brain. In doing this, I guarantee that you and your "mind" will (fortunately) never again be the same.

Andy, Bill, and Ann, Part I: Three Kinds of Visualization

Here are three true stories to show you how this works in real life. Each illustrates one of the three types of visualization. Now that you know something about the right-brain–left-brain relationship, you'll have some clues to what's going on.

Andy was ten years old with a severe case of asthma when his family sought the help of Dr. Gerald Jampolsky, a well-known California psychiatrist. Andy had been in medical treatment for a number of years, but it had succeeded only in keeping his symptoms "manageable."

On his first visit with Jerry, who uses visualization in his practice, Andy had his first taste of what he calls "crazy trips." To those of us accustomed to stethoscopes and drug prescriptions in doctors' offices, it was, indeed, a crazy trip. Jerry explained to him exactly what the bronchi looked like and told him that he actually could aggravate his attacks by seeing with his mind's eye his bronchi getting tighter. Andy was then sent home with instructions to try to have a much *worse* asthma attack!

On his return the following week, Andy told Jerry that he thought he would like to get rid of his asthma. Grinning sheepishly, he confessed that making it worse didn't feel good. In that week he had discovered that *he* was in control of his asthma. If he could make it worse, then he could also make it better.

Jerry and Andy then focused their work on seeing pictures of the bronchi opening and the asthmatic attacks receding. Within a short time, Andy was miraculously free of the symptoms that had plagued him.

Bill, at thirty-two, is the associate dean of a large university. He believed that because the man newly appointed dean disliked him it was just a short time until he would either be fired or have to resign. During a visualization, the image of his superior came to him very clearly. He saw his boss in his office, sobbing, with a helpless and frightened expression on his face, and then burying his head in his hands. This image was in stark contrast to the way Bill had described the dean to me.

His superior looked at Bill and pleaded with him, "Please don't try so hard so fast. It scares me." He explained that he was fifty-seven-years old and wanted a chance to succeed. "*You*'ve got lots of time," he told Bill. He added that he had just seen his doctor, who told him that he wasn't in very good health.

Bill was astounded by this response, so different from his conscious impression of a powerful and angry man. He also knew that he had touched the truth, which was later confirmed, about his employer's state of health. From these pictures he was able to see his own behavior in the situation in a new light. He saw himself as pushy, ambitious, and arrogant, with little concern for those he worked with.

Bill's visualization was the beginning of very important and beautiful changes in his relationship to his work.

Ann had a deep fear of falling. Every winter she, her husband, and a group of friends vacationed at a ski resort in Switzerland and so, with some reluctance, she had taken up skiing. With a lot of help from her teachers and friends, she had become skilled enough to ski with the others. But her fear plagued her, and the annual trip became a battle between her will, which was fiercely determined to conquer the fear, and her terror, which undermined not only these efforts but also the pleasure of the whole experience.

Last winter Ann used visualization to help herself. At a friend's suggestion, she began her inner movie with a journey to the top of a distant and remote mountain. There she found a building that resembled an exquisite Greek temple. She knew that inside this temple was the solution to her problem. With some trepidation, she entered and walked in. Waiting for her was a lovely woman dressed in a Greek toga whom Ann saw as her own special goddess.

When she asked the goddess for help to deal with her fear of falling, she saw herself floating. This was in contrast to her usual sense of herself barrelling and crashing down the slopes. Her goddess told her that she should carry this new image with her, and that it would help.

Somewhat skeptical, Ann nevertheless visualized herself floating down the mountain on skis before she fell asleep that evening and again when she awakened. To her utter amazement, the next day she skied substantially better than she ever had before. She felt herself actually floating. Not surprisingly, that was the beginning of the end of Ann's fear of skiing.

What these three adventurous people have in common is that they all used movies-of-the-mind to change their lives in very specific ways. Andy used his inner pictures to *heal;* Bill used his to *know;* and Ann used hers for guidance to *create a different reality.* While they all did this through images, they each worked with their images in different ways.

What Andy did is called *programmed* visualization. By deliberately seeing his bronchial tubes on his inner movie screen, either in a diseased or healthy state, he actually affected their condition—and with it the condition of his entire body.

We can use this same approach to program virtually anything we want. By visualizing very precisely whatever changes we want and then seeing our life as we want it to be, we can heal our bodies, have our dream house, get the job we want, improve a relationship with someone we love, and even win a championship sports event. There's undoubtedly a miraculous quality about images used in this way, which is why skeptics may have some difficulty dealing with it! But, as you will see from the dozens of true stories reported throughout the book, programming inner pictures does indeed do what it promises.

The revelations that came to Bill were through the use of *open-screen* visualization (also known as receptive visualization). In this type of inner movie, a question is asked or a theme established (in Bill's case, his job problem), and the pictures are allowed to emerge spontaneously on the open, or blank, inner screen.

We use *open screen* for all kinds of knowing and remembering. We can recall long-forgotten events from our past, as far back as our infancy, and discover answers to our most pressing current problems. We can also discover (as Jane through her orangutan did back in Chapter 1) what the truth is for any situation in our life. This type of visualization gives us access to a very deep and reliable wisdom.

Ann's experience is essentially one of *guided* visualization. When she climbed the mountain and met her goddess, she was following a given *scenario* rather than allowing her inner movie camera to wander of its own will. *Guided* visualization is used to spark the imagination by setting the scene, mood, and whatever other circumstances seem appropriate.

The message Ann received from her goddess was a classic *open screen*. Ann then went on to *program* her message—the image of floating down the mountain—which, in turn, created an entirely new real-life experience. You can see by this example that the different types of visualization can be used separately or together, in a variety of arrangements. Although they're useful in understanding visualization, in practice the distinctions fade and ultimately become unimportant.

What Happened to Andy, Bill, and Ann, Part II; Or, What Actually Happens in Visualization

Each of our starring threesome began their movies-of-the-mind by using a relaxation exercise identical or similar to those described in Chapter 4.

This first, essential step quiets both the mind and the body. As we have already seen, as long as the chatter of our thoughts fills our minds, nothing else can emerge from it. The body is equally involved in the thinking process, strange as that may seem. As long as it remains busy—whether in activity or simply by holding muscles tense—it also takes our attention away from what's going on inside us. The quiet state we achieve this way is the same as that reached by meditators. It not only serves as a door to our inner theater, taking us beyond the boundaries of our personality, but it also allows us to be wonderfully receptive to whatever we might experience there.

Mind Power: How It Affects the Body

Andy's miraculous recovery from a crippling disease seems less astonishing when we understand how the mind and body work together.

We see and accept their interaction when, for example, we look at erotic pictures and become sexually aroused, or when we become frightened and feel our hearts pound. Since our feelings are controlled by the right-brain, these responses give us a clue to what might occur with inner pictures.

Although the research in this field is still in its infancy, we've already found that visualization has a definite effect on the body's EEG, or electrical field. Physiologist Edmund Jacobson has shown, for example, that if you *imagine* yourself running, small but measurable amounts of contraction actually take place in the muscles you use for jogging.

Anatomists have demonstrated that there are pathways between the part of the brain where our pictures are stored and the autonomic nervous system which controls such so-called "involuntary" activities as sweating, blood pressure, and digestion. These same pathways link the autonomic nervous system and the pituitary and adrenal cortex. The end result is that a picture in the mind has an impact on *every cell in our bodies.*

That the mind and body are one inseparable unit is being proven in many different ways.

The research in biofeedback caused a revolution when it showed that the so-called "autonomic" nervous system isn't autonomic at all. We found that we could have absolute control over the parts of us we once believed totally out of our control—the rate at which our hearts beat and our brain-wave patterns, for example. We could go about learning how to alter these functions in much the same way as we would learn to ride a bicycle.

We've also been finding that certain kinds of personalities are more apt to get certain diseases than others. For example, the research reported in the book *Type A Behavior and Your Heart,* by Meyer Friedman and Ray H. Rosenman, shows that very aggressive, restless people who constantly feel under the pressure of time are the most likely candidates for heart disease. This is just one more piece of evidence that we are, indeed, what we think and feel.

From other disciplines we are finding that the tensions in our bodies are a response to our emotional life experiences. Many of those who go through Rolfing, a series of ten very deep massages, actually report the release of old memories and feelings with the release of tight muscles. When pressure is put on a part of their body, a picture of a past—and often painful—event comes to mind, along with a marvelous sense of letting go. Bioenergetic therapy is another approach to the mind through the body. By working on the body's defense system, or "armor," it seeks to free the personality trapped in it.

Still other evidence about the way our minds and bodies work together comes from those who read "auras," the radiating light that surrounds the body and is understood as its energy field. This halo-like light can be photographed with special techniques, and can be seen with the naked eye by some people. We find that the aura's color and tone change with mood. My friend Barbara, a recently divorced physicist who is investigating the aura with a team of researchers, called me the other day to say that she was falling in love with a marvelous man who she knew was equally smitten with her. When I asked her how she could be so certain about him, among the things she told me was that his aura was rose, the color of a state of love, whenever they had been together!

And those who have experienced acupuncture, which releases blocked energy, know that their sense of well-being is directly affected when their energy system returns to its natural flow. This energy has been understood and worked with in many different cultures over many years. It is known as *chi* by the Chinese and *prana* by the Indians, and is usually understood as the body's life force.

If Andy's recovery now seems almost routine, just wait (until Chapters 6 and 7) to see what *else* the mind and body can do together!

Mind Power: How It Affects the Universe

Bill's and Ann's experiences reported a few pages back involved *knowing* and *changing* things that seemed to be outside themselves. Bill knew that his boss was sick; Ann completely changed her experience of skiing. Further on, you will meet people who use movies-of-the-mind for such things as increasing their income, winning in sports, and finding the pet or house or car that is exactly what they've wanted.

We discover in these experiences that we, and we alone, have the power to create what we want in our lives. We can make every moment of every day a miracle! We affect the world, and the world affects us, through the power of thoughts and images. This is so because:

Our beliefs about ourselves and our world govern all our experience.

Our images are self-fulfilling prophecies.

What we envision in life is what we get.

These statements may be some of the most important things for you to ever know—both to get the most out of your movies-of-the-mind and to get the most out of life. Learn them well and live by them, and you'll find that your life begins to work!

We know the relationship between image and outer reality not only from observation. Now we also are getting confirmation of the mind's power to affect the universe from scientists, and especially from research being done in the field of physics.*

Through our inner images, our mind is causing what happens to us *all the time.* Whatever we experience in our lives— whether happy or unhappy, or good or bad—is the direct result of these images. The problem is that we usually are totally unaware of them, and so we don't see their connection to the events they cause.

The power of movies-of-the-mind comes from *deliberately* making our images conscious, and then *deliberately* programming the images of what we want. In this way it becomes possible to create what we *really* want in our lives.

Having said hello to our mind, we can now go on to learn how to channel its power.

---

* A very clear but simple explanation of how physicists view this process—in fact, all so-called metaphysical events—can be found in the delightful "picture book" *Space-Time and Beyond,* by Bob Toben in conversation with Jack Sarfatti and Fred Wolf. For those who want to pursue the subject more deeply this book includes an excellent bibliography.

4

How to Do It: You and Your Own
Private Screening Room

In the realm of the mind, what you believe to be true is true.
—John Lilly, M.D.

You already know how to direct the movies of your mind, even though you may *think* you can't. You do it all the time. In fact, everything that happens in your life is connected to your positive and negative inner images. Since you're probably not very aware of most of them, you also have few—or most likely no—expectations or disappointments associated with them.

In making your inner pictures *conscious,* which is what you're learning to do here, you can realistically expect a lot. Some of the things that you can expect are:

• To improve the quality of your life in exactly the areas that need improvement.
• To find new ways to solve your problems and make decisions.
• To be healthier, wealthier, and—believe it!—wiser.
• To increase your learning ability and improve your skills.
• To expand your creative talents.
• To help yourself get well when you're sick.
• To know what you need at any particular moment.
• To re-experience your childhood.

- To stretch your imagination.
- To break out of the tyranny of your intellect into the freedom of your intuition.
- To deepen your feelings of love.
- To sharpen your perceptions.
- To discover your own special strength and beauty.
- To experience other dimensions of yourself so that you can go beyond all your present limitations.
- Best of all, simply to feel good.

To Begin with . . . Set the Mood

You need no special experience, training, ability, equipment, type of mind, personality, or any other quality that isn't shared by everyone else in order to visualize.

You need only be who you are.

Being just you in a positive frame of mind, you are now ready to give over to your inner self, to a different state of mind, to a new way of listening and looking.

The state you will create is one of *receptive stillness*. Another way to describe it is *relaxed attention*. In this state, you are alert and concentrated on what is happening inside you. At the same time, you are *uninvolved* with what may be happening outside you, in the range of your senses.

Although yogis can meditate in the midst of chaos, most of us need to create quiet in our outer space in order to connect with our inner space. And so *my first suggestion is that you choose a time and place for your visualizations in which you won't be disturbed and you can let yourself relax.* Put aside, for the moment, your everyday activities and concerns. Allow yourself the heavenly pleasure of letting go of your thoughts and the tensions in your body.

There are very few *musts* in this book, but relaxation as a first step to visualizing is one of them. The more you slow your brain waves, the more relaxed you become, the more you can tune in to your own higher intelligence. Letting go into relaxation is like dimming the lights in a movie theater. Both let you see the images on the screen.

While you are visualizing, you may find that other thoughts come into your consciousness or that your mind may drift to other things. If so, simply bring yourself back to the subject of your concentration. The more focused you can remain, the better. I would suggest, however, that you not become so relaxed that you fall asleep, or so focused that your body and mind become rigid. You can't visualize in either of these states.

Once you are relaxed, focus your inner eye on your inner movie screen. You may discover or create a screen like one in a movie theater, or one to your own specifications, or you may not see a screen at all but know it is there by the pictures you see. Some of you will experience images in your head, either toward the back or in the center of the forehead between the eyes. For others, the images will seem to emerge from your solar plexus. And still others may experience them outside the body in the space in front of your closed eyes.

In this, as in everything else about movies-of-the-mind, there is no right or wrong, good or bad. Your experience simply *is*.

Finally I suggest that you approach your visualizations expecting a wonderful experience. It can be an exciting adventure if you let it be. And if you believe it will help your life, it will.

Relaxing: Three Ways to Quiet the Mind and Body

If you meditate, whether you use TM, yoga, the relaxation response, or any other discipline, you already know how to reach a state of relaxation. Or you may have developed your own system for relaxing when you're tense or to help you fall asleep; you could use that here as well. If you do not know a relaxation technique, you may use one described in the following pages.

The object of these relaxation scripts is to concentrate the mind and detach you from the inner dialogue that is with you continually. The essential differences among the three are that one approaches relaxation mainly through the body, another focuses on breathing, and the third evokes memories of good feelings.

These relaxation exercises can be done by yourself or with either a partner or leader reading the directions. You may also, if you want, record one of these scripts on tape, to later play back to yourself.

Each exercise begins with taking a deep breath from the abdomen. After doing the exercise several times, your body will begin to associate the opening breath with the feeling of relaxation. Eventually you will need only to take a few deep breaths, without going through the entire exercise, to feel deeply relaxed.

The best posture for these relaxations is either seated or lying down with feet uncrossed, hands loosely at your sides, and back straight.

Script I: Relaxing the Body

Close your eyes. Get yourself comfortable, and concentrate on your breathing.

Pay careful attention to your breathing. Recognize how slow and deep breathing will help to induce relaxation. Exhale. Then take a deep breath in through your nose and blow it out through your mouth. Breathe from your abdomen, deeply and slowly.

As you concentrate on your breathing, focus your attention on an imaginary spot in the center of your forehead. Look at the spot as if you were trying to see it from inside your head.

You will begin to realize that your eyelids have become tense. Get a sense of how tense the eyelids can become as you stare at the spot so that you can compare this feeling with relaxation.

When your eyelids become strained and uncomfortable, let them drop. Notice the feeling of relaxation that radiates all through and around your eyes. Allow that feeling of warmth and relaxation to move out to the temples and across the forehead.

Let the relaxation then radiate to your scalp, to the back of your head, to your ears, temples, cheeks, nose. To your mouth and chin.

As you feel all the tension leave your face, relax your jaw muscles. Let your jaw open slightly, so that all the tension can smoothly flow away.

Relax the muscles in your neck. As you do, let your head tip forward gently so your chin just about touches your chest.

Let this feeling of relaxation flow down into your shoulders and from there into the muscles of your arms and hands, then down your back, over to the front of the chest, on down to the abdomen, and then allow it to reach all the way down to the base of the spine.

Let the buttocks go completely loose and limp. Allow the warmth and relaxation to spread to the thighs, on down the legs, down to the ankles, and down through the feet to the tips of the toes.

Now you feel completely relaxed. Take a moment, starting from the top of your head and working down, to check to see if any part of you is not yet fully relaxed.

If you find any part of your body not fully relaxed, simply inhale a deep breath and send it into the area, bringing soothing, healing, relaxing, nourishing oxygen to comfort that area. As you exhale imagine blowing out right through your skin any tension, tightness, or discomfort. By inhaling a breath into that area and exhaling right through the skin, you are able to replace tension in any part of your body with gentle relaxation.

When you find yourself quiet and fully relaxed, take a few moments to enjoy it.

Script II: Deep Breathing

Close your eyes. Get yourself comfortable.

Pay careful attention to your breathing. Recognize how slow and deep breathing will help to induce relaxation. Exhale. Then take a deep breath in through your nose and blow it out through your mouth. Breathe from your abdomen, deeply and slowly. Allow your abdomen to rise and fall as you breathe.

With each inhale and exhale, count your breaths. Count *one* on the inhale and *two* on the exhale. Focus only on the breath and your counting.

If a thought comes into your mind which causes you to lose track of your counting, just return to the count.

If a thought comes into your mind, look at it as though it were someone else's. Neither grab hold of it nor chop it down. Neither stop it nor pursue it. Simply watch it come into view and disappear. Then continue your counting.

Count your breaths until you feel deeply relaxed. Breathe in and out slowly, counting each breath, until you feel quiet, relaxed, and still alert.

Script III: Remembering*

Stretch.

Take a good deep stretch, all through your body.

Slide down in the afterglow of that stretch, into a relaxed position.

Holding that afterglow feeling, reflect back on how it feels to be relaxed, as if you were in bed at night on the edges of sleep (though this time you stay awake and don't miss the fun). If you

---

* This is borrowed from Win Wenger's Psychegenics training.

are already trained in some form of meditation, reflect back on one of your *best* experiences of meditation and how that felt. If you are religious, reflect back on how it feels to listen in prayer.

Whichever experience you reflect back on, remember it more and more completely. Remember more and more clearly what it feels like, what elements in the experience go along with that feeling.

Remembering an experience re-creates the mental and physical basis of that experience. This is why you are already virtually back in the quality of this experience you are remembering, this experience you are remembering more about, more and more clearly.

While remembering the feeling and quality of this experience, now slowly breathe in deeply and breathe out deeply, 3 to 5 times, and just let your muscles go a little more with each breath out, relaxing more deeply.

Become more aware of what you are feeling and experiencing within you, and become more aware of your surroundings. It's surprising how much of a mental picture you can build up of your surroundings, just from what you can hear.

Taking about six seconds to do so, breathe in slowly and very deeply.

Exhale as slowly and deeply. With your lungs empty, try to blow out an imaginary candle a foot in front of your face—that's how deeply you should exhale.

Go on inhaling and exhaling as deeply as you can, very slowly, six seconds or longer each way.

Choosing the Movie That's Right for the Moment

The lights fade. You have a sense of darkness, perhaps emptiness. Gradually you notice something. A form. Some movement. Your inner camera turns toward it. It's not quite clear yet but you sense what it is. You focus on it. The scene becomes brighter. Ah, there it is. Not at all what you expected. Interesting. But not especially meaningful. You're tempted to open your eyes and forget the whole thing. But you're curious. You decide to go with it. Things begin to happen. It's fascinating. Also, a little scary. You don't know where it's all going to go. You suddenly realize that it's *your* movie and you can do anything you want with it. You decide to *really* let go into it. How strange . . . Incredible . . . You wonder what would happen if you added to the scene . . .

This is what I often see and feel when I begin a visualization. Since it's a fairly common experience, it might be your own as well. But you might also have a very different kind of experience. Part of the fascination of movies-of-the-mind is that they're spontaneous and unpredictable. They're also as different from person to person as you and I are.

The important thing for you to know is that there is very little you need do after you get ready to visualize by relaxing and becoming receptive to your images. There are, however, different ways in which you can experience this process.

Most of your movies will be a combination of receptive and progammed visualization, with one predominating.

As we saw in our encounter with Andy, Bill, and Ann in the last chapter, *receptive visualization* starts with a theme (Bill's problems with his boss) and then lets the movie roll of its own accord. *Programmed visualization* holds a positive picture in the mind in order to create the pictured situation (Andy's bronchial tubes becoming normal), or what it symbolically represents (Ann figuratively and literally floating down the mountain).

How to Tune in to Your Inner Drama

In *receptive visualization,* you let go into the images and allow whatever comes up to simply be there. It might be sights, sounds, or other sensory images, or it might be feelings, or both. You do this without judgment, without insisting on any particular result and without censorship.

If you don't immediately understand the meaning of the experience, you may seek through the images themselves a meaning that you *can* understand. You can question them, change them, look for a further response and add or subtract anything that occurs to you. You can put yourself into the movie, take yourself out, rewrite the script, and create entirely new situations. When you introduce specific images, you are using *programmed visualization* as well.

If you are visualizing for a specific answer or insight, you will get to know very clearly when it comes. It will feel utterly right. You will have no doubt about it at that moment, and so you will have a sense of resolution and deep satisfaction.

Sometimes what you sought in a visualization during a moment of quiet comes to you at another time, in another place, and in a form very different from what you expected. I have often asked to understand the meaning of an event in my life, or for guidance with a problem, only to have the answer days later. Then it will come in a sudden inspiration, or new idea, or feeling, or through a word someone says to me, or through something I read. I used to think that it was just a coincidence. Now I see it as the delayed finale to my movie.

Another way to use visualization is to re-create experience. You can go back in time to a situation of your childhood. Or recall an event or people or feeling from a more recent time in your life. Or remember information that you need at the moment.

You can also create an original experience. You might perceive your parents in a way you never have before. Or you might discover a special place within you that is soothing, loving, and peaceful, to which you can return again and again for nurturing and replenishment. The possibilities are infinite, as you yourself have infinite resources.

How to Program What You Want in Life

Programmed visualization may be used for different kinds of goals. They might include healing, teaching yourself a skill, rehearsing a coming event, creating new circumstances in your life, or experiencing something more subtle, such as a trip into the cosmos. *It is the deliberate use of the power of your mind to create your own reality.*

I would like to say at the outset about this incredible process that there is nothing too insignificant or too grand for you to visualize. *Our lives are limited by what we see as possible. In visualization, we expand what we have by expanding what we want.*

A basic rule of visualization is:

You can use visualization to have whatever you want, but YOU MUST REALLY, REALLY WANT WHAT YOU VISUALIZE.

This may strike you as strange at first. "Of course," you might say, "I want what I want." "Of course you do," I answer, "but is there also a tiny part of you that *doesn't* want what you want?"

However much you may *think* you want to be free of sickness, or to own a new car, or to succeed at a work project, or to fall in love, it's possible that you haven't yet created these things because *a part of you doesn't want them.* You may or may not feel deserving of what you want or deserving of satisfaction in general. You might be afraid to change things in your life, as a new romance, a new level of health, or even a new car would do. Or you might have a deep stake in *not* having what you want. For example, being sick may bring you a lot of attention, or keep a dependency going, or prevent you from resolving another issue in your life.

It's even possible that you know, deep down, that what you believe you need isn't *really* what you need. You may think that having a lot of money, for example, will give you the happiness you yearn for, when right now there's something much more fundamental missing in your life.

The less conflicted you are about your goal, the greater the creative power of your inner movie. And so you may have your best success at first with simple things.

For example, my friend Margot visualizes taxis emerging from dark, empty streets when she's returning home late at night. She has no conflict about wanting to get home quickly and safely, and, invariably, taxis appear where taxis are rarely known to cruise.

Another friend visualized a house down to the precise floor plan, and then found and purchased it the following week. He was very certain of what he wanted for himself and his family here, but he has had less success visualizing changes in his business, because of unresolved conflicts there.

A patient of mine had been visualizing weight loss for some time without effect. Through a visualization we found that she ate continually to cut off from her sexual feelings, which disturbed her. And so, her movies-of-the-mind, both for information and programmed, began to focus on her sexuality. She has now begun to lose weight.

The Twinge Effect

How will you know, you might ask, whether or not you really want something?

One way that you will know I call the *twinge effect*. When you are visualizing, you begin to sense that something is off. You sense a countercurrent to what you want. I sometimes feel it as a physical *twinge* in my body. Others sense a voice that might say, "Uh-uh. That's not for you." A patient described his twinge effect as the same feeling he had as a child when he reached into the cookie jar.

There are many ways to feel or know the *no,* and you will discover your own. If you sense that it is there, it is self-defeating to push it away and continue with your movie. Unless you experience a clean *yes* to what you want, the insidious *no* will undermine your best efforts.

A second way to know that there are countercurrents to your imagery is simply because it doesn't work. Although *it is important to allow time* for your inner pictures to become manifest as reality (perhaps a long time with something as complex as reversing the course of an illness or changing careers), if you feel there is no movement, it may be important to take a fresh look at your visualization.

Plotting the Plot

Formulating what you want is the first step in programming your movie. This is like the first draft of a script. In *conceiving* it, you consider the new experience, or goal, as a *possibility.*

Discover, first, what it is you want. This might require some outer research, if it is something material you want (a house or car, for example), until you know its details and flavor. Or you might want to *try on* or *try out* your visualization on your inner movie screen and adjust it as you look at it. An athlete might do this when rehearsing a skill or for a competitive event. An architect might explore a new design on his inner screen.

Another way to develop the theme and variations of your visualization is through your inner movies themselves. See what you want for yourself on your inner screen and sense how it feels. Is that really what you want? Does something else have to come first? Is there a *no* that needs to be explored? Are you comfortable with it? Have you left anything important out? And, most important, *does it feel good and right?*

You'll know. You'll know in a different way than you're used to knowing things. If it is right, you'll simply have a sense of the rightness of it. This knowing is a wonderful resource that you have within you. As more and more you get in touch with it, you will find it invaluable in every area of your life. And as you deepen your ability to visualize, so will you deepen your sense of what is right for you.

The pictures should be as *clear* and *specific* and *real* as you can make them. There is value in visualizing yourself happy. But there is far greater value in visualizing changes in specific things about your life that will contribute to your happiness.

The visualization might focus on the *process,* the *goal,* or both process and goal. To be successful delivering a lecture, for example, you might see yourself looking wonderful and feeling relaxed before the lecture, review yourself actually giving the lecture, see a responsive and pleased audience, and maybe even see a positive report in the next day's newspaper.

With illness, you might visualize what needs to happen in the body for it to heal itself. It is important with this type of inner movie to be certain about what occurs in the body in both the diseased and healthy state. Your visualization can also be to see and feel yourself healthy and whole.

The essential ingredient in programmed visualization is to *form in your mind a very precise and clear picture of what you need and then hold it, affirm it, and see it as being yours.* As you will see shortly, you back up these images with the strength of your positive will, thoughts, and feelings.

Producing and Directing Your Programmed Movie

Each one of the following steps is necessary to the success of this process, and shouldn't be bypassed. If you find one or several of them difficult, explore why and use them in a later visualization.

1. The first step, as in all movies-of-the-mind, is to put yourself into a relaxed, receptive state.

2. See the images of your visualization clearly and in detail. Concentrate on them. If your mind wanders, bring it gently back to your pictures. Change or modify or expand them in any way that feels right at the moment.

3. Become aware of the feelings you associate with the pictured goal. You might feel a yearning, or a soft and sweet melting, or excitement, or peacefulness. You might become aware of your heart beating quickly or notice sexual feelings or sense movement in legs or arms. Let both your body and mind experience whatever is there.

If negative feelings come up—fear, anger, anxiety, or irritation, for example—it is important not to push them away. Experience them. Look for what is causing them. At this point it would be valuable for you to concentrate on these negative feelings and explore them or challenge them. They may point to a countercurrent that is undermining the positive visualization. They may indicate that you need to deal with another aspect of your life first. Or they may be the reemergence of an old, habitual *no* to expansion, growth, and satisfaction.

Sometimes saying no to your *no* and standing by your right to pleasure and success will move you through this place. Sometimes the negation is deeper and more persistent. In that case, using visualization can help you find out why a part of you resists or rejects what you think you want.

4. Experience the movies with your other inner senses. Listen for sounds. Use your sense of touch. If it seems appropriate, smell or taste what you find in your movie.

The more complete the experience, the more aware you are

of both the sensory and feeling components, the more power you give to it.

If you find yourself unable to visualize a particular feeling or experience, it is usually a signal that a part of you is defended against it. As you work through the defenses, either through visualization or in other ways to expose the negating thoughts, the pictures will then be able to emerge.

5. Tell yourself in words, or send into yourself the thought, that you *deserve the very best* in life, and especially the state or object or goal that you are visualizing.

6. *Trust* and *believe* that you will have what it is you want. This last step is essential, although it may be the most difficult for some of you. The positive *belief* serves to motorize the visualization.

Believing means that you must give this process an honest chance. You need patience, as it may take time to manifest, and a willingness to accept that there are many possibilities below your consciousness and beyond the limits of your present experience. You also need to consider that what may appear to be coincidence isn't. *This is a live process* of cause and effect, of consciousness creating reality.

As with all things in the universe, there are both active and receptive elements of visualization. The active element is your *concentration* on the images. The receptive element is simply *allowing* them to work. Working *on* them is unproductive.

Other Things You Need to Know

Not only is it essential that you really *want* what you visualize, you also need to put your *will* and *energy* behind your visualization. This means that you should be open to doing whatever you need to, to get what you want.⌐

For example, when a sculptor looks at a piece of stone and sees its potential form, he is visualizing. But visualization alone will not create the sculpture. The artist needs to go through the steps—chipping away at the stone—that will materialize his vision. Conversely, without the vision no amount of chipping will create a work of art.

If you want a loving relationship, you may need to give up your stake in being detached, or "cool." If you want to be healthy, you may first need to put up with the discomfort of the healing process. If you want to live in a magnificent house, you may need to go out and get a job or get a better job than you have now. If you want to change your lifestyle, you may first need to go through a period of uncertainty and insecurity. These experiences are like the cost of admission to the movie: necessary and fair.

Another thing to consider when using visualization is whether or not it is in the best interest of you and those it will directly affect. What is *really* good for you will not hurt others, although in some cases it might seem that you have to choose between their good and yours. Visualization is a powerful tool and should be used with love and care. To abuse it is to abuse yourself and your world.

Also, I suggest that you visualize something that you know to be possible. I have a friend not quite five feet tall, with delicate features and fair coloring, who yearns to look like Sophia Loren. I suppose that if we can accept the power of the mind to cure terminal illness, we might expect that it could also cause other drastic changes. But, clearly, that's not where we're at here. Movies-of-the-mind is a way to help you expand your life experience and to deepen your experience of yourself. To use it otherwise may not be impossible, but it certainly is irrelevant and might conceivably be destructive.

As with Everything Else, There Are Pitfalls

You're fully sold on movies-of-the-mind and decide to give it a try, but the first time you do it you fall fast asleep. Or nothing happens. Or something happens, but you can't make head or tail out of it. Or you find your thoughts going a mile-a-minute and you never seem to get beyond them.

These are the movie-of-the-mind pitfalls.

Everyone has the experience at one time or another, even those who have done it for years, of setting out to visualize and not getting very far. It's very tempting to put yourself down for it. Don't! Although movies-of-the-mind are remarkably easy to do, they're not *that* easy. It might take you a few tries, maybe even more. We're all terrific at being busy or involved with things around us—TV, the telephone, the refrigerator, to name just a few—but are total novices at being still and looking inward.

Give yourself a chance to learn how to direct the movies-of-your-mind. It's a cop-out if you tell yourself that everyone else can do it but you can't. You *can*. And you *will*. Your pictures are there and they want to be seen. Let them be. This is a process of *letting go* to something, not *making* it happen.

When you're first starting out, you may want to choose themes which are fairly simple and which you're not ambivalent about. Mind Control graduates, for example, are known to use visualization with great success to find parking spaces! But this might be another pitfall to keep you from the full benefits and pleasure of visualizing. You're the only one who can know what's best for you. Maybe what's best is to do both kinds of inner movies. Some of my most moving and helpful experiences came during my first "trips."

Another thing you might want to do is to direct your movie with a friend, having her or him read the script to you. This may help you give over to your inner self more comfortably.

If you do have difficulties getting started, I urge you to stick with it. It's really worth it! However great the all-time greatest box-office hit might be *(Gone with the Wind?),* it's got to be a poor second to your own inner movies, once you get the hang of them.

What You Can Expect Once You Get Going

Anything and everything, simultaneously and separately, may come up for you when you direct the movies-of-your-mind. You may get very precise, *realistic images.* Strange and exquisite *symbolic forms.* Pictures that may either be identical to or very different from familiar objects, places, and people. *Words,* either that you can read or that you can hear. *Sounds,* both familiar and unfamiliar. A *sense* of something, unaccompanied by either images or words. An *intuitive knowing,* sometimes in the form of a flash. Or an experience different from all of these and that is uniquely yours.

Whatever it is, be with it. Observe it. Accept it. Feel it. Enjoy it. Know that it is as real as what is in front of your outer eyes.

What may come up for you sometimes might make you uncomfortable. You may perceive an aspect of yourself that you don't like. You may receive an answer to a question that doesn't suit you. Your negativity in a particular situation may loom large and unappealing. Or you may feel feelings that you erroneously believe are unacceptable—anger, helplessness, hatred, or sadness, for example.

Memories of past events that were and remain painful may emerge. As might dark thoughts and figures or scenes of unhappiness.

It is important to allow these pictures onto your screen and to accept that they are a part of you. Realize that it is they which create your negative reality. When you bring them to consciousness, you defuse their power over you. This is so because what you don't know exists within you cannot be examined or changed. Bringing what I call your *lower self,* the destructive aspects of your personality, to light is the first step toward transforming it. The second step is simply to accept it (everyone is negative and immature in some ways) knowing that it is just one very human part of yourself.*

Also be aware that we all have resistance to knowing ourselves as we really are. Abraham Maslow put it this way: "There is the need to know and the fear of knowing." I would add: There is also the need to change and the fear of changing.

I want to say unequivocally that in experiencing your inner world, it is far more likely that you will discover very beautiful, very moving, and very meaningful images. It is here that you will find your *higher self,* which is the very best that you are. Not only may you find the answers to your most searching questions, but you may also experience profound inspiration. Probing the inner dimension may also be a deep esthetic experience, incredibly revealing, sometimes very funny, and always fascinating.

The journey into the self is very much like the adventures of our mythical heroes, from Odysseus to Superman. We start out with courage and hope, curiosity and excitement. At times the trip is hazardous; at other times, ecstatic. At the end of the mythic journey there's the reward: the Holy Grail, the pot of gold, a soul-mate to love. At the end of the "inner" journey there's a far more wonderful gift: the discovery of the richest part of our being.

---

* I would like to say here that the process of visualization is utterly safe. In tapping the deepest resources of your mind, you can only *expand* your experience of yourself and life. If what you uncover makes you uncomfortable, you may choose to go through the experience of discomfort to get to its source, and in that way release it; or you may choose to turn off your home movie for now, perhaps to experience the uncomfortable image at another time.

5

Create the Life You Want for Yourself

Argue for your limitations and sure enough, they're yours.
—Richard Bach, *Illusions: The Adventures
of a Reluctant Messiah*

What you can visualize, you can have. The question is: Do you know what it is that you want?

Stop and think about that for a moment.

When you have some answers, try your hand at the next question:

What is it that's keeping you from having what you want?

If what you come up with has to do with "circumstances beyond your control," other people, bad luck, or anything else in the victim category, stop immediately and begin again.

Unless you can see that *what's keeping you from having what you want right now is . . . you,* it's almost impossible to get in life what you really want.

Visualization is a way to get what you really want in life. And one of the most important ways it does that is by having you, the visualizer, be responsible for your *possibilities*. You do this by fully accepting that the images you deliberately program have the power to change your reality.

I want to digress briefly here to point out the difference between visualizing and fantasizing. Although they seem alike because they both use inner images—usually about things which we would love to have in our lives—one is a powerhouse of creativity and the other tends to stagnate our potential.

The main difference between them is in the *intention* we bring to them. When we program movies-of-the-mind, we make a *commitment* to get what we want and we *trust* that we can have it. That means that we're prepared to follow whatever opportunities present themselves as a result of the visualization. And we know that we are responsible for making it happen. If it's a fabulous new job we want, we'll shape up our résumé and make appointments to see the right people.

Fantasies, on the other hand, tend to keep us stuck in our lives because they set impossible goals and absorb the energy that might otherwise go into programming what we can really have. Other people—or magic—usually take care of the hard stuff. The fabulous job we want comes to us in an unsolicited letter which offers three times the salary we're getting now, plus an annual trip around the world!

Fantasies, especially children's, are wonderful for shaping our imaginations. The fantasy (or reverie) state may also bring forth valuable insights. But it will not have the power to create new realities. That's the job of programmed visualization.

Here's How Programmed Visualization Works

Maryann, a pianist friend of mine, had begun to think of playing at one of New York's top cocktail lounges; her work, until then, had mainly been teaching music and accompanying dance classes, with an occasional weekend stint in a suburban night spot. In a visualization, she saw herself playing at the cocktail lounge of the Top of the Six's, a popular and chic midtown gathering place. A few months later, "completely out of the blue" she says, her agent called her to audition for that exact job. She told me this story the evening I stopped in to see her at the Six's. She was ecstatically happy and her performance was superb. I noted, in passing, the stunning outfit she was wearing. She laughed and confessed that it was almost identical to the one she had seen on her inner screen of several months earlier; she had "coincidentally" discovered and bought it a few weeks before her new job began.

John had been unhappy for some time about his job on a major metropolitan newspaper. He felt he was working too hard, not getting enough money for the time and effort he was putting into his work, and he felt ready to take on something bigger. He spoke with his boss about his discontent, but at that time there didn't seem any way to change the situation. John decided to set aside an evening to program a new situation that would be right for him. He listed all the things he wanted in a job. He then went on to list all the things he knew how to do. From this, he imagined a job title that summed up both what he wanted and was capable of doing.

Five weeks later, John was offered the precise job he had visualized. Although the position had never existed before, the title was almost exactly the one he had conceived and the responsibilities were exactly as he had imagined them. The hours and salary were also as he had programmed them.

Eric is a graduate student who had failed the final comprehensive exams at the end of his four-year program. He had been given the chance to take the exams again, but was afraid that again anxiety would keep him from doing his best. In a visualization, he saw the problem as a giant wooden block that stood in front of him. In programmed visualizations, he then saw the wooden block getting smaller and smaller. By the time the exams were scheduled, he was able to mentally reduce the block to a child's building block. In his visualizations he saw himself going into the examination room, felt himelf calm and self-assured, and carried under his arm the wooden block, now a mere miniature of the original, to remind himself of the power of his mind. He passed the exams this second time around with excellent scores.

Winning the Inner Way

While movies-of-the-mind are being used with great effectiveness in many different areas of life—for weight loss, vocational problems, to conquer fears, and to program positive relationships, for example—one of the most fascinating uses of visualization is in the world of sports.

Peter Karns, the coach of the U. S. Olympic Biathalon team, credits visualization with a vast improvement in his team's performance at the 1976 Winter Olympics in Innsbruck. This very difficult and exacting sport, which combines cross-country skiing with rifle shooting, is first rehearsed in the mind's eye in precise detail before it is actually performed.

"In our practice," Peter told me, "the competitors do deep breathing, then we lead them verbally through each tiny detail of the event while they picture it mentally, and finally we ask them to review each step mentally without any verbal direction. The repetition of the mental pictures is tremendously important for them to become completely automatic," he explains.

Karen Korfanta and Hank Taubler, coaches of the U. S. Olympic slalom racing team, use visualization to impress on each participant the course they will be skiing. These mental dress rehearsals review every bump and dip along the run, so on the day of the actual race there aren't any surprises.

Psychologist Richard Suinn of Colorado State University has devised a method he calls visuo-motor behavior rehearsal for his work with athletes. After a deep-relaxation exercise, he instructs those he is working with to review with their inner eye the skills and/or the course they will be using in competition. He told me that each athlete discovers for himself the exact imagery that works best for him. For example, Lyle Nelson, a member of the U.S. Olympic Biathalon team, first pictures the Rock of Gibraltar and then sees himself similarly steady before he sets off on his course.

The key to effective imagery, Suinn says, is the deep relaxation that precedes it. The visualization then is not only visual, but can be auditory, emotional, and muscular as well. He notes that many of the athletes "involuntarily" tighten the muscles involved in a sport while they concentrate on their inner pictures. His work with the Colorado State ski team substantially cut down ski errors and won it their league's trophy.

Another part of Suinn's technique is to have an athlete do a mental slow-motion run of an event, so each detail can be observed. He says that this can help someone pick up a slight error which had consistently been throwing him off.

The use of visualization in golf is explored in Michael Murphy's delightful *Golf in the Kingdom*. Like many others involved in sports today, he told me that he regards the game as a channel to something beyond it. "Golf is first a game of seeing and feeling," he writes. "It can teach you stillness of mind and a sensitivity to the textures of wind and green." He also sees the sport as a way to perceive how one plays the entire game of life, and to go beyond that to become more deeply in touch with the universe.

In teaching beginners to play golf, Michael starts with the essential specifics. He instructs his students on how to use visualization to keep their eye on the ball: "Imagine a golf ball. Make the image of it as vivid as you can. When anything intrudes upon the image, let it pass. If the golf ball disappears, imagine it again. If it wavers, make it steady. Doing this you can practice keeping your eye on the ball. You can practice in your room on a rainy day."

If you can't keep thoughts out of your mind while doing this inner practice, Michael suggests that you get to know the intrusion. "What does it show you about yourself and your situation in the world? Exploring the invader can be helpful to your game."

Michael Murphy is the director of the Esalen Institute in Big Sur, California, that harbinger of so much of what we have come to know about the mind and body in the past decade. And so it is not surprising that he regards the world of sport as a laboratory for the vast frontier of the New Age.

I should mention here that my own look into movies-of-the-mind in sports reflects a similar point of view. Athletes are, of necessity, pragmatists. Their use of a rather esoteric tool to improve their skills not only points up its effectiveness but also suggests ways to use visualization in very different fields. I also agree with Michael Murphy that what is happening in sports today may serve as a prototype of what will in coming years be happening in other areas—education, business, and politics, to name just a few that could use it.

The most popular of current sports, jogging, is also being enhanced by visualization. Mike Spino, a former college distance champion and now director of the Esalen Sports Center, coaches distance runners by combining a variety of tempos, styles—and movie-of-the-mind techniques. He writes in *Beyond Jogging: The Innerspaces of Running:* "Expanding the use of exercises to include the mental aspects calls for visualization techniques that enable the natural running consciousness to grow richer. These mental techniques could be as basic to conditioning as physical activities."

Using guided imagery, Mike Spino has those he works with reach a state of deep relaxation by first seeing a white light like a halo over their heads and then drawing the light into their bodies. He then suggests that they picture themselves on top of a rock, in a beautiful field, feeling serene and calm and warmed by the sun. "If you feel tension in a particular area of your body, or if you have a real or imagined injury in one area of your body," he tells them, "draw the light from the halo over your head to the spot of tension or injury."

Mike suggests other visualizations to be used while running to help the runner meet specific challenges. In the image he calls "The Big Hand," the runner sees a large hand along the whole of his back giving assistance as he runs. When fatigued, the runner imagines himself leaning into the hand.

Another visualization sees a skyhook holding the runner erect while it pulls the person over the ground.

A third visualization he uses successfully is to imagine a wire being extended across a football goalpost or spanning two trees. The runner then sees a harness across his chest and a wire connecting him to the wire spanning the posts or trees. He then lets himself be pulled toward the span by force, as if he were being reeled on a fishing line toward his goal.

"Visualization techniques such as these," Mike says, "will be among the most important aspects of athletic training in the future."

Timothy Gallwey, author of the bestselling *The Inner Game of Tennis,* also views the mental side of sports as at least as important as the physical side. "The theory of the inner game," he says, "is that your performance is dependent on the state of your mind. The real game is to learn how to reach that state of mind and stay in that state of mind in which your performance is best and your perception is at its clearest."

I watched Tim work at, of all places, a psychological convention with two people who had never before played tennis. He instructed them initially to simpy bounce and hit the ball, which they did for ten minutes with predictably awkward results. Then he instructed them to think of themselves as great tennis players. "You look casual and competent," he told them. "You have just won at Wimbledon. You are, indeed, Billie

Jean King." While we on the sidelines laughed, the players continued to play and get better and better. One of them later told me that she felt a big difference in her playing before and after Gallwey's instructions. After he suggested that she could play like a pro, she felt that she actually could!

While writing this book, I invited several friends of mine, all Sunday golfers with scores in the 80's and 90's, to experiment with visualization over a month's time. Some of them concentrated on seeing their strokes and others focused on the end result of the ball dropping into the cup. At the end of that time they each had cut their score by at least five strokes.

Money-Making and Mind Expansion

How, you might well ask (especially if your prime passion of the moment is other than sports), does all this relate to you changing the things that need changing in your own life?

My answer to you is that there is basically no difference between reprogramming your tennis strokes and reprogramming anything else in your life, large or small.

Movies-of-the-mind offers an entirely different way of getting what we want than most of us have experienced before. Instead of figuring things out with our heads—calculating, reviewing, memorizing, being "objective," trying, striving—our focus is turned inward to *seeing what we want as a current reality, and then simply allowing it to happen.*

John Robinson heads a multi-million dollar shipping company which sends automobile parts to every corner of the planet. He is a handsome man in his fifties, with a look about him that says he knows where he's at. His energy is staggering. The morning we met, he arrived at his office at 9 A.M., after a three-mile jog, and after having flown in from Thailand via New York to San Francisco just seven hours earlier. He is a living testament to the power of the mind to create a full and rich life.

John is one of increasing numbers of business executives who are using visualization in their professions. "Successful people," he told me, "seem to be able to combine the best of both parts of their mind—the rational and the intuitive—and recognize that both are important and valuable in their decision-making." He adds that he firmly believes we can control our own destiny through imagery.

John is so convinced of the value of movies-of-the-mind, that he scheduled a series of weekly meetings for his management team and invited a psychiatrist who uses imagery, Dr. Gerald Jampolsky, to work with them. In these sessions, they were taught a deep relaxation method and then explored their inner pictures about various business problems and relationships.

My long-held conviction that people in the "straight" world of business are less flexible than the rest of us yielded to a very different attitude when I learned about this work. These successful executives were, in fact, more open to going into the unknown than many of my professional colleagues!

Jerry Jampolsky led the program off with concepts which you're familiar with by now. "Ultimately, what you believe is what you become," he told the group. "The word *realism*, which so often limits your expectations, needs redefinition. What's real is that there are no limitations to what you can be and do. You don't have to know how the creative mind responds to your imagery. You just need to trust that it does."

He then suggested that each participant picture something that he or she wanted to accomplish within the business. "See it," he told them. "Believe it. A crack in the belief will prevent it from happening. Nod your head as though you were saying yes." From time to time he reminded them to notice what was happening in their bodies. "A body-mind relationship," he pointed out, "is essential for this process to work."

And so these people who had power over millions of dollars and thousands of employees visualized new ways of dealing with both old and new problems, human and corporate. At the end of their visualizations, they programmed the thought that they would look each day for opportunities to help others. In exercising the potential of their minds, Jerry told them, they activated a very vital part of themselves. Before ending the session he reminded them that in visualization you do not *make* something happen; instead you *allow* it to happen. With ongoing practice those who visualize could expect continually to increase their power. "Don't be surprised," he suggested, "if after a month you notice that your staff is working more effectively and with more energy, that the cash flow position is better, that problems which used to take two weeks to resolve get solved in two days, and that you have more and better ideas than you've had in years."

Tales of Picture Power

From my ever-growing collection of movies-of-the-mind which people have shared with me come those that follow. I offer them here as inspiration for your own visualizing. They may point to areas in which you can create new and wonderful experiences for yourself, or suggest images for you to bring into your inner movies.

Andrea was returning to the job market after twelve years as a full-time housewife and was finding job-hunting painfully frightening. To deal with the fear, she began spending a part of the evening before each interview imagining details of the following day. She would see herself enter the building, get in and out of the elevator, and give her name to the receptionist. Dressed in the clothes she planned to wear that day, she would see herself and the interviewer meeting and discussing her qualifications. When she felt anxiety come up, she would direct her body to relax. She would also rehearse some of the things she wanted to say. "The first time I did this," she told me, "I couldn't believe how relaxed and fun the interview was. And I really tuned in to the other person." Subsequent interviews were even easier. A few weeks later she was offered and accepted an excellent job.

Steve used a symbolic image to deal with a similar problem. Scheduled to speak on an interview television program about a subject dear to his heart, to which he hoped to win converts, he found himself paralyzed by stage fright. At a friend's suggestion, he began, a few days before his appearance, to picture himself as a giant magnet, drawing people in the studio and home audience to him. He admits that it's impossible to measure the effect of this visualization, but told me that he felt very comfortable speaking that day. In the weeks that followed, he also received a strong response in letters and phone calls to the ideas he had talked about.

Joan is a talented free-lance fashion illustrator who had always feared that she wouldn't be given another assignment after she completed a current one. She began a daily visualization of seeing herself working in her studio surrounded by the clothing she would be illustrating, speaking on the phone and saying, "Yes, I would love to do it. I'll be right over with my portfolio," and then seeing herself note in her appointment book the scheduled interviews. Within a week she began getting telephone calls from people she had never worked for, who had heard of her through other employers and artists. The more she programmed, the more she was able to let go of her feelings of insecurity about her work. Not surprisingly, her career also skyrocketed.

An especially favorite story comes from my friends the Bookers. The family had decided that they wanted a dog, but in following up ads in the local newspaper hadn't been able to find the kind of pet they wanted. They finally decided to come together to compare notes on the pup they each had in mind. As they talked it over, Mary, the mother, drew their ideas on a sketch pad. What emerged was what they all called a "doggie dog"—a spotted short-hair of indeterminate lineage which they agreed was just the right dog for them. A couple of days later they found a pup exactly like the one in the picture. But, sadly, he had just been promised to someone else. So convinced was the family of the power of their visualization that they left their phone number "just in case" and stopped looking any further. A week later the people to whom it had been promised changed their minds, and the dog became the Bookers'.

Joseph Murphy, lecturer and writer on the power of the mind, tells, in *Your Infinite Powers to Be Rich,* of a salesman who felt he needed a $50,000 annual income to meet the needs of his family. Every morning for three months he stood before his mirror after shaving and told himself, with feeling: "John, you are a tremendous success. You are making $50,000 a year. You are an outstanding salesman." During this time he took up public speaking, which led to his being asked to give a talk at his company's annual sales meeting. As a result of that speech, he was promoted and given a more lucrative district at a larger annual salary. At year's end, his commissions and salary exceeded his wished-for $50,000. "Truly the mind is the source of wealth and all the riches of Heaven," he wrote in recounting his story.

And, finally, the use of visualization for weight loss must be included among the little miracles we can create with our mind's eye.

Like many people who have weight problems, Bob long had an image of himself as overweight and regarded eating as his number one pleasure. Now, as soon as he gets up in the morning, he says to himself: "My body only keeps the food that I need. I'm getting thinner and thinner." Then he visualizes himself looking healthy and energetic. He has dropped thirty pounds so far by using this technique alone.

Jean, a veteran of diets, was never without her calorie-counter—or her craving for hot fudge sundaes. Every morning she now visualizes herself wearing the "thin" clothes she loves and feeling herself slender and light. Soon after she began this program, she told me, she found herself unable to finish what she served herself at mealtimes. Unlike her previous attempts to lose weight, there was no discipline involved, no having to say no, nothing she needed to do except continually mentally affirm her inner picture of herself slim.

Cindy, at forty-five, is one of the most gracious and glamorous women I have ever known. Three-and-a-half months before we met she had weighed fifty additional pounds. She had lost the weight through relaxation and visualization, and in the process changed her entire life. "My life at the time," she told me, "was an endless round of busyness. I had no communication with my husband, a rotten sex life, a bratty ten-year-old son, and too many volunteer commitments. The only pleasure I had in life was when I was in the kitchen preparing food and eating it." As she used movies-of-the-mind to deal with the problems in her life, her fixation on food progressively disappeared. What Cindy did was to visualize three times a day each of her immediate problems and then to place each one in a balloon and watch it float away. As her awareness of her life deepened through both receptive visualization and psychotherapy, so did her commitment to letting go of those things that kept her from having what she really wanted. Her "new" body is a beautiful outer statement about her new inner state.

In each of these cases, visualization became the way for someone to create what he or she most wanted in life at that moment. And so it can for you. There is no limit to what you can have through movies-of-the-mind. And there is no area of your life that can't be helped and expanded by it.*

* NOTE: Directions for doing programmed visualization are given on pages 40–46. I urge you to go back and reread those pages before beginning your own visualization. Although the process is extraordinarily simple you should understand it fully before beginning it.

6

How to Discover the Message of Your Dis-ease

Health exists when body and mind function in harmony.
—Kenneth Pelletier, Ph.D.

As the split between the mind and body begins to be mended in the practice of medicine, the healing arts are flowering like a garden in June.

In Berkeley, California, the once taboo notion that all disease is psychosomatic comes out of the closet. A medical center directed by some of the most prestigious names in medicine and psychology calls itself The Psychosomatic Medicine Clinic. Their brochure tells a newcomer, among other things, that to prevent pathology "an individual needs to be considered physically, psychologically, and spiritually" and in "relationship with his total environment."

At the nationally famous Cancer Counseling and Research Center in Fort Worth, Texas, patients are taught to meditate and visualize to strengthen their immunological systems.

At UCLA's Pain Control Unit, 200-odd patients are treated with acupuncture, biofeedback, hypnosis, meditation—and "pain classes" where they hold dialogues with their inner "advisers."

And, in Marin County, California, the medically supervised

Center for Attitudinal Healing offers terminally ill children and adults programs that teach them how to voluntarily control their "involuntary" systems.

However bizarre it might seem, this is the wave of the future. The new medicine begins where the old medicine left off—with the patient's own power to heal himself.

Mind Over Matter: A "New Medicine" Case Study

Nancy is a thirty-year-old mother and elementary school teacher. After months of wracking pain in her abdomen, a few years ago she agreed to undergo a hysterectomy. But the pain persisted long after the operation. She also developed a post-operative infection. The antibiotics prescribed for her eliminated neither the infection nor the pain.

In desperation, Nancy contacted a doctor who used therapeutic visualization. On her first visit, instead of trying to control the pain itself, the doctor focused on why the pain kept returning. He helped her reach a state of deep relaxation and then suggested that she go in her mind to a place that was peaceful and beautiful. There she was to invite whoever or whatever was causing the pain to visit with her. Then she was to ask what it was that he or she wanted from her, and try to come to an agreement which would relieve the pain.

For several days Nancy visualized with no effect. The notion of what she was doing frightened her. She was angry at the doctor for not making the pain go away and she wouldn't consider that she, herself, might have that power. Finally, out of overwhelming pain and frustration, she gave in to the process she had begun.

The person she saw with her inner eye was the infant she had miscarried a few years earlier, in her fifth month of pregnancy. An autopsy at the time had found nothing wrong with either the baby or herself that could explain its death.

At her doctor's suggestion, Nancy asked the baby if it was responsible for the pain in her abdomen. When it answered "Yes," she then asked what it wanted from her. The answer was direct and explicit. The baby told her, "I want your life for my life."

Nancy felt a profound sadness, but she was not surprised. She had long been convinced that she had willed the baby's death because the pregnancy was unwanted; it had come too soon after the birth of her first child, at a time when she felt emotionally depleted.

She then entered into a continuing dialogue with the infant, In the first days, still driven by guilt, she was defensive toward it. But she soon recognized that the image was the offspring of that very same guilt. And so she began to stand up to it and challenge it.

"Before my eyes," she says with awe, "the life force began ebbing from the image. When it was finally gone, I opened my eyes and saw a red light in my abdominal area, followed by a powerful flash of pain moving out of the side of my body." As the red light receded into the sky, so did Nancy's pain. Permanently. In deciding to give up her guilt toward her unborn child, she was able to let go of the pain which was the physical manifestation of it.

The Patient Becomes a Bodymind

Nancy was a patient of Dr. Martin Rossman, one of a growing number of doctors using visualization in their medical practice. Attractive, brilliant, and in his early thirties, Marty Rossman is a graduate of one of the nation's top medical schools and a thriving three-year practice of what he calls "traditional medicine." During that time, he says, he saw hundreds of patients come and go—and not get well. Disillusioned by his experience and convinced that there had to be a better way, he left his practice to work with Dr. Irving Oyle at Oyle's experimental medical center.

It was there that Marty learned how to help patients help themselves. He saw that the only way to look at disease was from the patient's personal experience. Sophisticated diagnostic tools might help a doctor understand a patient's symptoms, but he found them useless for getting to the real root of the problem. He returned to San Francisco with a new point of view and some unorthodox new techniques. One of these was visualization.

Marty approaches illness as a symptom of disharmony or stagnation in the entire body-mind system. He believes that through the mind we have control over the body. We can influence *the way* it grows, *what* grows, and what *doesn't* grow. In Nancy's case, traditional medical therapy couldn't work as long as she was unaware that her mind had a stake in holding on to the pain it had created.

This is a very different way of looking at sickness and health than we're accustomed to. It assumes things that are both as old as mankind itself and revolutionary. These old/new concepts allow us to consider ways to heal that go way beyond anything most of us in the West have ever experienced.

The doctors I met with who are practicing what is known as *holistic medicine,* and who are teaching their patients self-healing techniques that include visualization, have certain assumptions in common. Not all agree with all these notions, but they all agree with at least some of them.

Basic to the new approaches to healing is the belief that *the mind and body are one inseparable system.* That means that everything a person thinks and believes and feels is experienced in his body.

We all know that when we are embarrassed, we may blush; and when we feel bored, we yawn. More subtle relationships show that certain types of personalities and behaviors are associated with certain diseases.*

If we can accept that thoughts and beliefs take root in our bodies as well as in our minds, then it is just a short step to considering that *if we deliberately change our thoughts, we may deliberately change our bodies as well.* This, as we'll soon see, is the basis for using movies-of-the-mind as a tool in healing.

Other assumptions which are related to the above are:

• *Our belief systems—especially the way we see ourselves and the universe—have a direct relationship to our health.*

• *When we change our belief systems, we change the condition of our health.*

• *If we can recognize that we have a part in creating our illnesses—through our thoughts and beliefs—then we can accept that we have a part in creating our own wellness.*

• *Healing is most effective—and perhaps only effective— when we are active and responsible participants in our own healing process, instead of passive victims of either the disease or the treatment.* This is in sharp contrast to the way we usually experience being sick, which is to go to a doctor and let him do his thing—surgery, injections, X-ray therapy—to our unprotesting and uninvolved bodies, or to stay home and let the disease do *its* thing.

A Confrontation with Cancer

Perhaps the most dramatic use of these ideas is in the work of Dr. Carl Simonton and Stephanie Simonton, who are using

---

* Doctors are finding a relationship between the onset of cancer and feelings of deep helplessness set off by the loss of someone close. Extreme aggressiveness and restlessness has been linked to heart disease. The book *Psychosomatics,* by Howard and Martha Lewis, documents relationships between repressed rage and ulcerative colitis; difficulty crying and asthma; superachievers and ulcers; and having been very responsible and "grown-up" as a child and hyperthyroidism. These relationships just hint at what's becoming known in a burgeoning field.

visualization along with traditional medical therapy on patients with terminal cancer.

The Simontons accept for treatment only those patients who are willing to take responsibility for their disease, that is, who will look at what was happening in their lives that led to the disease and will then do whatever is necessary to make themselves well.

The Simontons' approach is twofold. Those who come to the Fort Worth clinic work individually and in groups with Carl and Stephanie to explore what may have caused the disease and their reasons for wanting to live—and die. They are also taught a deep-relaxation exercise similar to the one on page 34, after which they visualize; they do this three times a day. In their movies-of-the-mind, they see their cancer and then imagine an army of healthy white blood cells swarming over it to carry off the malignant cells. The white cells flush out the malignant cells and the patient then sees himself as healthy, with his immunological system working perfectly.

Patients have reported seeing the white blood cells become a knight in shining armor on a white horse, or a crab, or a frogman in a black wetsuit. If they are receiving medical treatment at the same time, the cobalt rays or pills take on symbolic roles in the mental warfare.

The movie-of-the-mind script must see the white blood cells as strong and powerful, and the cancer cells as weak, confused, and easily destroyed. One patient's cancer grew despite regular visualization. It was discovered too late that he saw the cancer as a huge rock, the treatment as a stream of water, and the white blood cells as tiny scrub brushes. A part of him felt helpless and didn't really want to get well, and this is the way it showed itself.

The Simontons insist that their patients look for the answer to the underlying question, "Why did I need my cancer in the first place?" They also ask their patients to look for meaning in the location of the tumor. For example, the professional singer must ask himself why he developed throat cancer.

Why and how do these visualizations work? The Simontons have found that a person's active imagination can discover the cause and then create the cure for his or her own cancer. The mental pictures are so powerful, in fact, that they can prod the body's immunological system into destroying even the most widespread malignancy.

Two "Incurables" Speak About Their Cures

Several former patients of Dr. Simonton, who reported incredible cures, have spoken of their experiences.

Dorothy, a fifty-one-year-old social worker, was bursting with energy and looked like an ad for healthy living when we met. Five years earlier she had been diagnosed as having incurable cancer of the colon and was on the brink of death when she flew to Texas to meet the Simontons.

She spent nine days on their ranch. There she learned certain relaxation and deep breathing techniques. There she learned, too, why she had created her disease. She saw that there was a part of her that really wanted to die. After her father's death, she told me, she found her life unbearable.

She quoted a line of Goethe's to me. "Whatever you can do, or dream you can, begin it." Working with the Simontons, she began to see that she could choose to live.

Dorothy started using visualization in the Simonton program. In one of her movies, she saw the cancer cells as hamburger meat and the white blood cells as barking dogs tearing the meat apart. In another, she saw herself as a ship's captain continually locating and sending healing energy to the problems within the boat, which was her body. She would send white blood cells to the lining of her stomach and direct them to handle the problem.

At the time I talked with her, Dorothy had survived her cancer twice as long as predicted, and there is now no sign of the disease in her body. She still relaxes and visualizes three times a day for twenty-minute periods. In the visualization she sees her white cells engulfing cancer cells, as an amoeba engulfs its food. When I asked her how she felt, she beamed. "Better . . . stronger . . . healthier . . . and happier than ever before in my life," she said emphatically. Looking at her, I didn't doubt it.

Bob is a dynamic and successful business executive who is the very image of good health, and looks much younger than his forty-two years. At the time he found his way to the Simontons, he had been given less than a one-percent chance to live.

Before he went to Texas, he says, he was resigned to a quick death. He was overwhelmed by pain from cancer of the groin and was constantly sick from the chemotherapy. At the Fort Worth clinic, things miraculously began to change. The changes seemed directly related to his thrice-daily meditations and visualizations.

Six weeks later Bob returned to his personal physician for a check-up. Although the only therapy he was involved with at the time was the Simontons', the cancer was found to have shrunk 75 percent. Bob says that two months later his doctor couldn't find any disease in his body. And six months later, he adds proudly, he won a racket ball match from the North Carolina state champion.

Within Each Sickness Is a Message

These seeming miracle cures are the application of mind over matter. But they are not simply wish-fulfillments. Dr. Simonton, along with other physicians doing visualization therapy, views disease as a potentially valuable aspect of our life process. Within each sickness is a message we need to decode and learn from. So another belief of the new medicine is:

Illness is not necessarily bad for us—and may actually be good for us—since it can be taken as an expression of some imbalance in our lives. If we understand and respond to its message, it is potentially regenerative rather than necessarily degenerative.

As Dr. Rossman described it to me, each of us has an aspect of ourselves, the intuitive part, which knows how to exist in harmony with our mind, our body, and our environment: how to breathe, eat, work, play, and love without conflict. Illness, he says, is a cry from this part for change. It causes old forms to break down as a prelude to the emergence of something new—much as puberty is both a death and a rebirth. And so illness may actually become a death-reversing process.

"When you stop the death of an old pattern, you stop the healing." He adds sadly, "Some people are more willing to die than they are to let their beliefs die."

Looking for the Meaning

A number of doctors encourage their patients to enter into a dialogue with an archetypal or mythical figure which they discover in themselves. The purpose of this dialogue is to find the meaning of the disease—what the physical symptoms represent—and then to point the way to release through a reordering of the person's life.

"The body is often the battleground in the struggle between conflicting ideas and attitudes. The symptom may represent one aspect of the conflict," Marty Rossman told me. "Once a person is willing to have a dialogue about the conflict, it changes form."

Dr. Irving Oyle, with whom Dr. Rossman trained, sees the function of the doctor as guiding a patient to the realization of his or her fullest and highest possible state of consciousness. Like the alchemists who are his spiritual forefathers, Dr. Oyle believes that the power of the visual image to totally transform life experience is a vital healing tool.

I met Irving Oyle one spring evening on a houseboat in Sausalito, California, where he was giving a lecture on how the mind participates in healing. Far from the halls of academia, it seemed an especially appropriate place to explore new aspects of holistic medicine, especially with someone who gave up—as he had—a twenty-year traditional practice among the Eastern medical establishment to pioneer new ways of healing in the "New West."

Dr. Oyle uses both traditional and new systems in his practice. He works with acupuncture *and* prescribes antibiotics. He uses sonopuncture (high-frequency sound) *and* sets broken bones. But the most interesting part of his practice—to me, at least—is his use of movies-of-the-mind.

Dr. Oyle helps his patients deeply relax and then asks them to go to a lake and wait for an animal or figure to appear. This animal, or figure, he says, will tell them precisely what in their life they have been doing to stimulate the symptom. He explains this as a person's connection with God, the universe, the other side of the brain. He explains it further:

"When a winged fairy, a butterfly, or a wise old man appeared in the mind's eye of a human primitive, he or she did not question the experience. In those days, the stuff which was going on inside your head when your eyes were closed seemed just as real as the goings on inside your head when your eyes were open."* Today, people with vivid dreams or active imaginations, he says, are being told to stamp these inner visions out in the name of mental health!

Following scores of successes using this technique, Dr. Oyle

---

* Irving Oyle, *Time, Space and Mind* (Millbrae, California: Celestial Arts, 1976).

suggests that the next time we feel an emotional charge or stub our toes, we don't name it or look for a reason, but instead, we meditate on the events and look for a message.

How It Works: A Doctor Talks with His Inner Dog

Dr. X is a young physician who had been cured of rectal cancer through surgery and massive radiation but was left with severe, continuing pain. He described his anguish as like a dog chewing on his spine. After several sessions focused on relaxing, he and his doctor went in search of that dog and found it.

At first, the dog wouldn't talk to him. His doctor suggested that as soon as the dog was willing to speak, the patient should ask it if it was chewing on his spine to get attention, and then ask as a demonstration of its power to take away the pain for just a few minutes.

The young doctor was resistant. But two days later he finally connected with the dog, who told him that he'd never wanted to be a doctor but that his mother had pressured him into it. He resented his mother, medical school, and his patients, the dog said, and the resentment was related to his getting cancer. Over the next few sessions, the dog began to advise him. By following its advice, Dr. X found that his pain soon moved into a controllable state.

Dr. David Bresler was this young physician's doctor. He is also the director of the UCLA Pain Control Unit, where sufferers of chronic physical pain come to seek relief. His patients have arthritis, backaches, headaches, stomach disorders, allergies, and an assortment of other ailments which defy conventional treatment. His goal is to find ways other than painkillers and surgery to bring pain under control.

"Under normal circumstances," David Bresler says, "your nervous system will turn off pain by itself. If it doesn't, it's because there's a message there. Your body is telling you something important that you're doing wrong with your life. Usually it's trying to tell you to stop doing something—such as worrying or being too self-critical or eating the wrong foods. So we think it's important *not* to administer symptomatic therapy like medication, but to really achieve understanding of why the pain is there and what's the message."

The UCLA Pain Control Unit uses a variety of techniques, including hypnosis, biofeedback, acupuncture, relaxation exercises, nutritional counseling, and family counseling. It also uses the kind of visualization that brought the young doctor with back pain in touch with his "gnawing dog" and other patients in touch with people and animals which guide and advise them.

In a group where patients meet to discuss their progress and, among other things, their advisers, a typical comment comes from a former Demerol addict. "The last time I talked with my adviser he said I need to have more pain so I'll continue working on myself. He said if I didn't have pain, I'd quit the relaxation exercises and be anxious again."

A Cyst, a Backache, and a Migraine Speak

This method of directing questions to your inner process—whether it be to an adviser or simply to the inner self—is invaluable in understanding where your life may be stuck at any given moment.

Mary had an ovarian cyst that was still small enough not to need surgery but large enough to worry her. In meditation it came to her that the meaning of the cyst was to point out that her in*sist*ence that things go a certain way in her marriage was destroying her. The cyst would per*sist* as long as she remained in*sist*ent. Mary was suddenly able to see her home situation very clearly, and began to expect less from her husband. While she began taking responsibility for her own pleasure, she continued visualizing the cyst shrinking. Within a few weeks, it was gone. (It's not unusual, by the way, for the symbolism of a situation to be understood through a play on words, as happened here.)

Karen was plagued with severe lower back pain. When she used visualization to see what it looked like, she saw two bright red muscles pulling at each other. The guide she brought to her consciousness was a young Indian woman, about her own age and "very loving and gentle." From her, Karen learned that the pulling of the muscles symbolized the pulling she felt in her life. She was continually pressuring herself to be "good" and to meet the expectations of everyone around her, from husband to co-workers. She learned to relax her body to relieve the stress in her back and to relax her rigid demands on herself to relieve the stress in her life.

And, finally, one of my favorite true stories—this one from Irving Oyle—is about the psychiatrist with migraine headaches who visualized a mermaid named Ethel to advise him. Not surprisingly, Ethel was far from his image of an appropriate adviser. He told Ethel about his reservations about her, in fact that he thought she was corny, to which she replied, "So sue me!" And in answer to his questions about his headaches, Ethel told him that not only did she know everything he wanted to know about them, but added that he deserved worse!

In contacting your own guide, be aware that a dialogue with your adviser is a reflection of what's going on inside you. If your adviser is sarcastic, as was the psychiatrist's, it probably reflects your own cynicism, as it did his. If your adviser acts timid or frightened, it may reflect your own timidity about going into your images. If your adviser won't talk to you, it may be because you don't want to know what's happening in you that's causing you to be sick.

Your intuitive system is continually trying to communicate

information to you. This visualization technique simply allows you to have access to that source in you, through a symbolic mediator. I should point out that there is no doctor anywhere who can make this work for you. It is your own dialogue with yourself, with that part of you that knows what's utterly best for you.

David Bresler suggests that people locate a man, a woman, and a child adviser. These figures are symbolic of certain aspects we all have, regardless of age or sex—the active and rational, the receptive and intuitive, the spontaneous and trusting. He also suggests that you be honest with your advisers and not make commitments that you're unwilling or unable to keep. "Treat your adviser as you would treat any valued, trusted friend," he wisely tells us.

Outrageous as these approaches to healing sound, they work. Not instantaneously—although, for some, the relief does come quickly. But over a period of time, for those who are willing to suspend their skepticism, a very powerful new ally becomes part of their lives. The advisers provide a continuing connection to the patients' hidden thoughts and beliefs. Through this channel they may have access to deep personal insights, information on how to relieve distress, protection when they're about to get into trouble, and the power to remove pain instantly.

My own adviser, incidentally, is a young bearded man who lives in a Swiss chalet at the top of a mountain. He helps me make decisions and advises me when I'm confused about something in my life. I simply ask him, "What should I do?" and then let the answer come. It never fails to help me.

Communicating with Yourself

In the following chapter we will explore some ways to use visualization for healing. But even more important than the healing process is an understanding of the meaning behind our ailments. And so here I offer some guidelines to help you get in touch with the messages within yourself.

To begin with, I want to remind you that *the limits of your beliefs define the limits of your reality.* For, this reason it is important that you allow yourself to be open to all possibilities. If your mind is closed to the notion of inner guidance, then no amount of visualizing will produce it. If you are open to finding an inner source of knowing, then—with patience and trust—you will.

The second point I want to make has to do with guilt and self-blame. While accepting that your illness is related to sub-conscious thoughts and beliefs is essential for healing yourself, it is also essential that you not blame yourself for your illness. Our diseases point to positive new directions where we need to go in our lives. Staying stuck in guilt serves only to keep us stuck in self-destructive feelings.

Third, I would like to mention that the consensus among those I spoke with was that if it is not in the best interests of the whole organism to overcome disease at this time, these techniques will not immediately eliminate the disease. Under-standing the message of the disease will, however, indicate where you need to make life changes, and become the first step toward a new relationship with your body and mind.

And, finally, these and the other healing techniques in this book should not be used apart from medical consultation. *If you are sick, then you should see a doctor.* What I suggest here is totally compatible with traditional medical therapies and may assist them in helping the healing process.

Your Adviser Script

Begin the visualization by becoming deeply relaxed. Using your own relaxation method or one from pages 34–38, allow yourself to totally relax your mind and body, so that you are totally focused on your inner screen.

When you feel yourself deeply relaxed, go to a place in your inner movie that is very beautiful and very peaceful. It might be a quiet, empty beach with waves gently billowing onto the sand. Or it could be a lovely meadow on a glorious spring afternoon. Or it might be a place where you've vacationed and where you remember being very happy and relaxed.

When you feel yourself very comfortable in this beautiful place, look around for a person or an animal. If you don't see it at first, keep looking.

When the figure appears, ask it to talk with you.

Tell it why you have come looking for it. Tell it that you need its help.

Allow yourself to be with this figure as comfortably as you would be with a friend in your own living room. It is a part of you. It is your own creation. It is benign. It is there to help you.

When you feel comfortable and accepting of your adviser, ask it the question you have been wanting to ask. Ask it to kindly tell you the message of your illness or pain.

Then wait patiently and receptively for the answer.

If an answer doesn't come immediately, ask your adviser how you can find the answer to your question.

Keep asking questions until you have the answers that you have sought.

When your answers come and you feel satisfied that they are what you sought, thank your adviser and tell it that you will return again to visit with it.

Allow yourself to come back into the here and now of outer reality.

Allow yourself to feel good and to feel that you have found out what you wanted to know.

Allow yourself to use the information you have received with wisdom and love.

Allow yourself to return to the beautiful place where you met with your adviser whenever you feel a need for guidance.

Allow yourself to know that you are giving yourself a great and important gift by discovering the message of your illness or pain.

7

How to Stay Healthy

Joy and pain are mutually incompatible.
—Dr. David Bresler

Glenn is eleven years old with a thatch of uncombed blond hair, a mouthful of braces, and big brown eyes that eagerly take in everything around him. A science-fiction buff, he also has a small golden ball which radiates healing light and energy, and which appears at his summons when he is in pain or ill. This golden ball resides inside him, visible only to him, emitting its golden rays only on his instructions. His family has never seen it but they know of it as witnesses to its effects. With his golden ball, Glenn has been able to quickly rid himself of headaches, bellyaches, swollen sinuses, and of pain from a gash that required half-a-dozen stitches.

Glenn's sister, Betsy, who's nine, routinely uses an est visualization* to get rid of headaches—her own and her friends'.

Glenn and Betsy's mother—my long-time friend and professional colleague—corroborates what her children have told me. She then confesses that in lieu of aspirin, she now eases menstrual cramps by visualizing cool, loving fingers gently soothing swollen ovaries. In lieu of laxatives, she has eliminated

* Described on page 97.

a lifelong constipation problem by visualizing the unrestricted flow of waste through her digestive tract. And in lieu of cold remedies, she relieves enflamed sinuses by visualizing golden light shining on and through them.

Neither in their lifestyle nor in their use of visualization for healing are these friends far-out. They are, in fact, just a very few among the many people who today are getting rid of aspirins and other medicines, relying on their own innate healing abilities to relieve sickness and return to health.

What Do We Really Mean by "Health" and "Sickness"?

Good health is a reflection of being in harmony with yourself physically, psychologically, and spiritually—and extending that harmony to your total environment. This environment includes your family, peers, job situation, and living situation. No doctor or medical therapy can do that for you. Your well-being is ultimately your own personal responsibility.

The word *health* goes back to an old Anglo-Saxon root meaning *whole*. *Heal* comes from the same root, as does *holy*. I strongly believe that the time has come for the notion of health as wholeness—as the balanced, harmonious functioning of the person—to reassert itself over our current notion of health as a response to drugs, surgery, or other medical therapy.

Against the new epidemics of chronic disease, in fact, medicine doesn't even seem very effective. For all the early intervention, the powerful drugs, the incredibly skilled surgery and the complex machines, life expectancy beyond infancy has not improved significantly in the past one hundred years. Cancer survival rates resist change; many heart attack victims survive as well at home as in coronary care units; and today's drug "breakthrough" has a way of becoming tomorrow's tragic mistake. In addition, as we increasingly hand over our destiny to specialized experts, our dependence on expertise creates a paralyzing sense of individual helplessness.

As health exists when body and mind work in harmony, illness appears when this process is disrupted. This disruption occurs most measurably in the presence of stress and conflict. Dr. Kenneth Pelletier, research psychologist at the University of California Langley Porter Neuropsychiatric Institute, points out that stress disorders have long since replaced the infectious diseases as the major health afflictions of the post-industrial nations. He lists among these diseases cancer, cardiovascular and respiratory disorders, arthritis, ulcers, migraines, and such lesser ailments as allergies, dermatitis, impotence, headaches, backaches, and colds.

We all have stress in our lives and much of it may be caused by or result from positive events. As Ken Pelletier says, "Life without the challenges which induce stress responses would be no life at all." A new house, a promotion, marriage, or any other change, positive or negative, can cause stress. When any stress, positive or negative, is prolonged, or combined with other stresses, we may start to see clinical signs of illness. And when it becomes very intense, we may begin to see severe organic and psychological pathology. The connection between the state of the mind and the state of the body is so pervasive, in fact, that Ken Pelletier says of his practice: "All disorders that I work with I consider psychosomatic."

What Can Happen When We Stop Worrying

If we want to learn how to get and stay well, we must first learn how to deal with the stress in our lives. We've already seen how to use our symptoms as a key to what's wrong— and therefore stressful—in our lifetyles. Here we look at "stress-reduction" as both a prevention and a treatment of disease.

In the last decade, we have seen the emergence of meditation, and especially transcendental meditation (TM), as a powerfully effective tool against stress. Following on its heels have come the Relaxation Response and a renewed interest in yoga.

Dr. David Bresler has an especially wonderful prescription for his chronic-pain patients. In addition to relaxation exercises, he prescribes *four hugs daily.* "Joy and pain are mutually incompatible," he says, and adds that he's found the hugs to be as effective as anything else.

Saturday Review editor Norman Cousins may have programmed the most original—and possibly one of the most effective—ways to use a positive state of mind to create a positive state in the body. When months of medical treatment for a severely painful and near-fatal illness failed to make any difference, he decided to stop all medications and prescribed for himself, instead, daily and large doses of laughter. He spent hours watching old tapes of "Candid Camera," supplementing this regimen with large amounts of vitamin C, and began his amazing return to health.

When we stop worrying and let go of the tension in our body by deliberately relaxing, the results are remarkable. All the body functions—blood pressure, respiration, immunological activity, to name just a few—relax and begin to work more efficiently. In this relaxed state the body's self-regulatory processes work at their best to produce optimum health and the feeling of being well.

It is no coincidence that it is also the state of relaxation in which we become highly attuned to our inner being and in which all the deep explorations and programming suggested in this book should be experienced. Thus, being relaxed not only brings us into harmony physically. It also brings us into harmony at every other level of our experience.

With the body in a relaxed and receptive state in which highly focused concentration is possible, we can then directly communicate with it to program very specific effects through visualization.

The power of the mind can actually create and re-create

the body and its cells. (Harold Burr, an anatomist from Yale Medical School, has shown that all the protein in the body is renewed at least every six months, and so not one particle of ourselves is identical to what it was six months ago.) Knowing this, we can change, eliminate, or add to what's already there. We can destroy malignant cells and make injured cells whole again. We can relieve pressure on a part of the body, unclog another part, raise or lower the temperature of still another part. We can protect ourselves from poisons and increase the healing effect of medicines. We can shift pain in the body around and move it out of the body entirely. And we can strengthen or weaken any part of us that we can imagine in our mind's eye.

How Formerly Sick People Programmed Themselves to Get Well

Margaret is a former patient of Dr. Martin Rossman, one of the "new" doctors who uses programmed movies-of-the-mind to change conditions in the body. At fifty-five, Margaret describes herself as "very ordinary" except for the fact that she has lived with severe pain from a tightened urethra since she was eleven. Until she saw Marty Rossman, her life had been a succession of visits to doctors and painful and expensive treatments.

Marty had never encountered a case like hers. "He didn't know if he could help me," she told me, "but he said, 'If you're not better by the third visit, I won't see you again.' I had never had that experience with a doctor before," she added with awe.

The visualization she evolved was based on her hand-drawn picture of a bladder. In her inner movie she used all the instruments all the urologists had ever actually used on her, in procedures that she had become expert at. Then she mentally filled her bladder with drops of water until it was so full that she thought she couldn't endure it any longer. By mentally stretching the capacity of bladder and urethra, the physical symptoms that had plagued her abated.

Margaret reruns her inner movie twice daily. It is now three years since her two-month visualization training and her condition remains completely normal. "I wrote my former urologist and told him what had happened, very tactfully, but he wrote back that he didn't believe me." With gentle compassion she adds, "I guess that he's just too old to accept new ideas."

George Frayne, the rock musician, is also a former patient of Dr. Martin Rossman. He came to Marty after an automobile accident had "messed up my back" and after he was almost arrested some months later because he was thought to be a junky from the effects of all the painkillers and tranquilizers he was on.

In a receptive visualization, George saw his back pain as an intricate knot. Then in the programmed visualization he devised he saw himself oiling the knot and slowly untying it, inch by painful inch. He has extended the use of visualization into other areas of his life, and uses it especially in his creative process. One of the conclusions he's come to from this experience is: "When they tell you in school to think, you should do just the opposite!" He was referring, of course, to quieting the left-brain logical mind in order to activate the right-brain intuitive mind.

Dr. Gerald Jampolsky is using healing visualization with both children and adults—individually and in groups—for ailments ranging from learning disabilities to leukemia.

After sitting in on some of his groups, I found myself especially moved and inspired by his extraordinary work with children.

Jerry told me that he works with the child "wherever he

is in his heart and mind," as well as with the images he may already have. One little girl, for example, loves rainbows and feels very safe under an image of a rainbow. The visualization they do together helps her expand her imagination about rainbows, and then allows her to use the images as healing agents.

In a group in which children deal with their cancers, Jerry begins, as he does in all groups, by directing them to put their "thinking" minds away. He then has the children draw pictures of how they see their disease in their "seeing" mind. Pictures drawn by one child appear on pages 88 and 89. These show very explicitly the youngster's understanding of the progress of his disease. Sometimes Jerry asks the children, point blank, to illustrate what dying means to them. These extraordinary pictures show both Jerry and the child where the child is in his sense of his illness and where deep beliefs need challenging.

Jerry feels that the sick children who come to him need to concentrate on living fully in the moment. Certain kinds of negativity, he says, keeps them stuck in the past or attached to the future. And so one of the visualizations he uses is to have them create a mental blackboard complete with chalk and eraser, and erase any of the following words whenever they enter into consciousness: *impossible, can't, try, if only, but, however, difficult, ought to, should,* and any other words that lead to comparisons that categorize or measure. Sadly, some of these children do die, but while they are alive the positive visualizations nourish them and give them a focus on the moment.

In a group for people with glaucoma, movies-of-the-mind take several directions. People in the group learn to love their eyes (many of them feel they developed problems because there was something they didn't want to see). After meeting with an ophthalmologist, they use his technical explanations to create such images as sponges soaking up the fluid around the

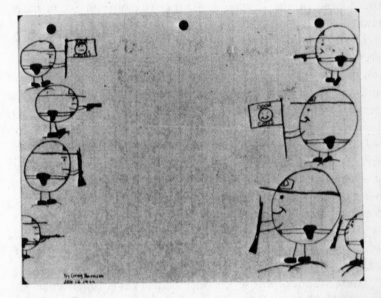

When Dr. Gerald Jampolsky works with children who have cancer, he asks them to draw the pictures they see in their minds' eyes. These three drawings were done by Gregory Cole Harrison at different stages in his disease. In the first picture, the "good cells" car is winning the race over the "bad cells" car. The "good cells" and "bad cells" fight it out in a boxing ring in the second drawing; the two are more equally matched here, and a referee is now necessary to decide the outcome. In the third drawing, the "good cells" soldiers are clearly larger and stronger than the "bad cells" soldiers, reflecting the boy's own positive feelings about his fighting for life.

eyeball. They also challenge in visualization their common belief that glaucoma inevitably leads to blindness. And they imagine whatever treatments and medical assistance they're receiving as beneficial and healing. The effect on reversing the course of the disease has been awesome in some cases, and at the very least impressive in the others.

David is one of the young people Jerry has worked with. At sixteen he was hit by a truck while riding to school on his bicycle, after which he was comatose for eighty-six days and was later told that he would never walk again. Over a period of months Jerry had him visualize himself moving, jumping, being balanced, doing all the things he might do with healthy legs. Today David is walking and back at school, and improving steadily. David told me that he applies his imagery in school and is now taking exams without feeling nervous. He visualizes himself actually taking the exam successfully, and then goes on to do it.

My files have begun to spill over with other such stories, which have come to me from doctors and former patients all over the country.

There's Janet, whose chronic backache is gone since she began visualizing the melting of the cement block that she saw in her back.

There's Anne, who cured herself of diverticulitis by visualizing the tense red area soothed and healed by an imagined golden ointment.

There's Lester, who with the help of Dr. Robert Leichtman, cured the severe itch and scaliness from five years of psoriasis by visualizing colored mists of red, green, blue, and especially gold, showering his body.

And there's Wes, who, in an est training, eliminated a very severe headache by moving it first outside and then back in, and left, right, down, and all around in his head. Once he experienced the power to manipulate it in any fashion he chose, he could then exercise his power to get rid of it.

And, finally, there's Herb, who, when hospitalized with a severe case of hepatitis, created a visualization in which half a dozen short men dressed totally in white continually scrubbed down the dark walls of his imagined liver. Each time a sponge came off a wall, it was a little black, and when the water in the pails turned completely black, it got thrown out a window in the liver and was then replaced. He directed this movie several times each day and ended it each time by seeing a powerful sunbeam fill him with cosmic energy. Herb's doctors predicted he would be sick for months. He was discharged with all tests negative seven days later.

Dr. Jeanne Achterberg, who has worked with the Simontons in using visualization with cancer patients, and Dr. Frank Lawlis, both currently doing research in physiological psychology at the University of Texas Health Science Center, are exploring and documenting the relationship between imagery and the course of disease. Among the things they're finding is that the way a particular illness develops and how much rehabilitation can be expected are *predictable* from a patient's inner pictures. They are also discovering that patients themselves actually have the ability to diagnose and prognosticate their diseases through this incredible tool. They are currently using this procedure for people with cancer, hypertension, and diabetes. The drawings from their work on pages 92–93 show how the patient "knows" what's happening in his or her own body.

As miraculous as some of these stories seem, they need to be seen in a broader context. All the patients using visualization under a doctor's supervision have been or continue to be in traditional medical therapy. Most, if not all, are simultaneously restructuring their lives in response to the messages of their diseases. And all are challenging deep, negative beliefs about

This drawing was done by a 34-year-old woman with a rare non-malignant type of breast tumor (her tumor weighed approximately eight pounds when removed). Her drawing shows the white blood cells as fish, probably piranhas, and the smaller ones she described as immature white cells. The cancer cells are the ones that look like jellyfish and, in scale, are the size of a silver dollar. At the time she drew this picture she was having a lot of pain and radiation treatments were not arresting the growth.

Drawn by a 54-year-old man who was a charity patient, and very unsophisticated about physiology and medicine, this picture portrays the condition of his brain tumor with amazing accuracy. He has also shown in rather accurate detail the phagocytic activity of the white blood cells.

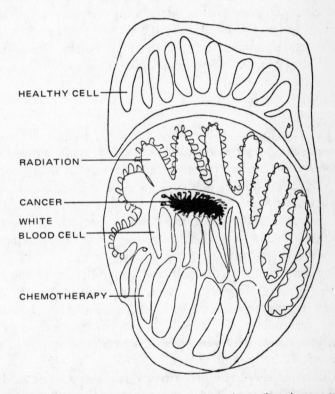

HEALTHY CELL

RADIATION

CANCER

WHITE
BLOOD CELL

CHEMOTHERAPY

This amazing drawing by a 49-year-old woman who had recently undergone radical mastectomy for breast cancer shows her need for further medical treatment. She sees that her white blood cells, which she portrays as small and slow-moving, aren't strong enough to conquer the cancer by themselves and need help from radiation or chemotherapy. The cancer itself is seen as a hairy black bug.

themselves and the nature of life so they can create healthy, happy lives.

What we've seen here, nevertheless, demands our attention and further exploration. It is my deep hope that these techniques, or others like them, will be part of our children's education so they can become aware very early of the power of their minds. I also envision introducing procedures that teach the control of the mind over the body to hospitals, senior citizen centers, and nursing and old-age homes. We all need the kind of miracles these stories of healing inspire!

Scripts to Use for Healing

First and foremost, the *most beneficial* thing you can do for yourself is to *learn and daily practice a relaxation or meditative exercise*. This is the most effective way to help yourself if you are not now in the peak of good health, and to stay well after you reach that state. If you follow none of the scripts in this book other than one of the relaxations that appear on pages 34–38, you will have given yourself a monumental gift worth many times this book's cost.

The very best visualization you can program is one that comes from your inner being. The "experts"—physicians, psychologists, myself—can at best offer guidelines to help you begin this process. It is really up to you to discover what only you know: why you have "dis-ease" and how you can again create body-mind ease.

All scripts should be preceded by inducing a state of deep relaxation and visualizing a place that you've experienced as beautiful and peaceful.

Note that these scripts can also be used by other people—just one other or an entire group—to help the healing process in a person who is sick. For example, a parent can do these visualizations with, or apart from, a sick child. Healing visualization done in a group can be a very powerful tool when carried out in the spirit of compassion.

Three Visualizations for Specific Ailments

1. Visualize *healing energy* circulating through and soothing the disharmonious part of you. This energy might appear as golden or white light, or in another form that you recognize as healing.

If your energy is low and you're feeling tired, depressed, weak or chilled, breathe in energy from imagined sunlight. If you're feeling hyperactive and restless, see your excess energy flowing out through your feet into the ground.

When you know that *heat* is an appropriate medical remedy (check with your doctor), visualize and feel warmth in the sick or injured area. This facilitates the flow of blood with its healing properties to the area.*

2. Visualize the *healing process*. This can be either symbolic or based on images from medical texts or X-rays.

Begin by picturing your disorder, mental or physical. Kenneth Pelletier says that if it looks exactly like what you expected, odds are that the image is wrong; it's more likely to be something completely unexpected.

Examine the picture in as much detail as possible. Then transform the picture into a positive image. See the disease actually healing.

Dr. Mike Samuels suggests, in his wonderful text *Be Well,* some examples of the healing process. They include erasing (or killing) bacteria or viruses, building new cells to replace damaged ones, making rough areas smooth, making hot areas

---

* Autogenic training, developed by Dr. J. H. Schultz, offers an excellent system of relaxation, breathing, and specific directions, usually involving visualizing cold or heat, for specific disorders. This system is described in detail in *Autogenic Therapy* by Wolfgang Luthe.

cool, making sore areas comfortable, making tense areas relax, draining swollen areas, releasing pressures from tight areas, bringing blood to areas that need nutriment or cleansing, making dry areas moist (or the reverse), bringing energy to areas that seem tired. The basic sensations of the healed state that you want to create are: smoothness, comfort, gentle warmth, suppleness of new tissues, moistness, resiliency, strength, and ease and harmony.

The visualizations that Dr. Carl Simonton and Stephanie Simonton develop with their cancer patients tend to be symbolic and dramatic. Knights in armor on white horses, for example, might rush at cancer cells with their spears to systematically destroy them. Or a ravenous dog might devour cancer cells that resemble hamburger meat.

Use your inner eye, your imagination and the anecdotes throughout the book to create your own visualizations.

3. Visualize a *state of wellness*. In this visualization, see the sick or injured part of you as healed and your whole person as radiantly healthy. See yourself as you wish to be: happy, energized, feeling positive about your life.

Recall yourself at the healthiest time of your life, with the added bonus of your present maturity. Sense how you were then: how you breathed, felt, moved, looked.

See yourself in this marvelous healthy state walking in the sunshine and feeling in tune with life. Know that this is how you *are*, right now, just beneath the symptoms that mask your wellness.

In the mystical tradition there are many variations on the theme of seeing the self immersed in a brilliant white light, or bathed by the rays of the sun, which represent the universal energy which is our life force. This visualization can have a very powerful healing effect.

Three Visualizations for Relieving Pain

1. Use *noise-removal breathing* (see page 100) to wash the pain out of your system.

2. Visualize the pain diluting and diffusing throughout the body, and then leaving the body through the skin.

A variation on this is to breathe in with each inhalation soothing, relaxing nourishment and breathe out with each exhalation the tension, tightness and discomfort. Each time you inhale, bring twice as much healing oxygen into your system. Each time you exhale, remove twice as much tightness, pain, or discomfort. Actually *see* the pain leave.

3. Focus very closely on your area of pain. Then experience its geometric shape. Then see its color. And then estimate how much water it could hold if it could hold water. Repeat these three steps until the pain is gone. *It works,* so don't give up when it hasn't seemed to work after a few go-rounds.*

Visualizations to Assist Medical Therapy

Keep in mind that all healing is ultimately self-healing. The most superb medical attention is finally worthless if someone doesn't want to be healed. Conversely, the most mediocre medical attention—or perhaps even none—can bring phenomenal cures if the patient actively participates in the healing process.

Here are some suggestions for how you can help whatever medical therapy you may be receiving:

1. Visualize the medical treatment you are getting doing exactly what it is supposed to do.

For example, visualize the drug that's been prescribed for you moving through your bloodstream to the site of the disease, and then doing what it's meant to do—such as destroying viruses

---

* This technique is adapted from one used in the est training, where it is known as the "headache process." est recommends it for minor aches and pains only.

or depressing the pain receptors. It would be helpful for you to find out exactly how the drug you're using works in the body.

2. If you are receiving a treatment such as physical therapy, massage, or even radiation, you can help it by simultaneously visualizing the process working. Allow yourself to be receptive to its healing effect. See it doing what it's supposed to do.

PAMPFA: A First-Aid Visualization for Injuries

The Journal of Clinical Psychology (January, 1975) carried an impressive report by D. H. Schuster, an Iowa State University psychologist, on how visualization is being used to reverse the psychological effects of medical traumas. The procedure is called PAMPFA, an acronym for Psychological Assist to Medical First-Aid.

By repeating the behavior at the time of the accident in the mind's eye, the patient removes the ill-effects of the emotions associated with the upset. If, for example, you've burned your hand removing a hot skillet from the stove, you review in your imagination all the things that happened just before, during, and after the accident.

This reduces the fear associated with the event and again focuses the patient on the injured part he's avoided because of the pain. This very fear and avoidance unconsciously block the healing by decreasing the blood flow to the hands, feet, and injured part of the body.

Pick a time interval surrounding the injury, say five seconds before to ten seconds afterward. Following one sensation at a time, review this time interval. Include such sensations as pain, awareness of injured part, temperature, sounds, words, actions, attitudes, and thoughts.

Go over the same time interval, being aware of all the sensations at once, as they actually happened. Repeat the action in your mind's eye and in pantomine, if necessary. Pay particular attention to thoughts and attitudes in this total sensation.

Repeat steps one and two until the pain stops or greatly diminishes. This may take five minutes to an hour.

Build up an awareness of the injured part and see it having been healed and normal again. Repeat this frequently during and after the emergency assist.

Scripts for Staying Healthy

The following three movie-of-the-mind scripts are to help you feel a general sense of good health and well-being. They can be used both when you're ill and when you're well, for healing, and to feel terrific when you feel just pretty good.

The Energy-Flow Visualization*

This movie-of-the-mind is based on the Chinese concept of *chi,* or life energy, which circulates into and out of the body from the earth and cosmos and flows through it along prescribed circuits (called meridians) in an ever-continuing cycle.

Begin by relaxing your body and breathing deeply from the abdomen.

When you feel relaxed, focus your eyes inward and begin to see energy streaming through your body, warming you, vitalizing you, energizing you, cleansing you.

As you inhale bring a wave of energy up the front part of your body, beginning with your toes and moving to the top of your head.

As you exhale see the energy move down the back of your body, out the back of your heels and into the ground.

The energy may take the form of golden light or be a vibratory

* Based on a visualization developed by Dr. Irving Oyle.

sensation or resemble a flowing brook or molten lava, or be a series of lights successively turned on. It makes no difference if your image is very similar to, or very different from, these; *whatever you see is your unique and accurate perception of your inner process.*

Continue to circulate the energy with each deep inhalation and exhalation.

As you observe the energy circulating through your body, be alert to areas of tension and blockage. Direct the energy to penetrate those places, to unblock them and soothe them.

Allow the energy to massage every part of your inner body.

When you feel soothed, relaxed, and revitalized, open your eyes and return to the here and now of physical reality.

Noise-Removal Breathing*

Begin by relaxing the body and breathing deeply from the abdomen. The exercise on page 37 is an excellent lead-in to this one.

When completely relaxed, and as you *inhale,* imagine you have a nose in your feet, a nostril in the bottom of each foot, between mid-arch and the sole of each foot. Imagine as you breathe in deeply that you are pulling in air up through your feet.

Feel as if each breath coming in through your feet and up through your legs and body is swirling up through the tensions, toxins, tiredness, and other noise that had been cluttering the tissues and cells of that part of your body. Feel your breath swirling through and carrying away all that unwanted stuff. Feel your exhaled breath carrying that noise out of your body, carrying away anything that doesn't belong.

Feel your *exhaled* breath to be laden with that stuff you are pulling up and carrying out of your system, so much from your system just pouring into your breath that your breath begins to

---

* Based on a visualization developed by Win Wenger for Psychegenics.

actually *feel* warm and rich. That extra warmth and richness is felt especially near the end of your exhaled breath, so really push that noise out of your system by exhaling very deeply.

As you pull noise up from your body and push it out with your exhaled breath, you are not only cleaning up your system but doing a good thing by creating a lot of new life energy.

Keep noise-removal breathing very deeply, pulling noise up and loosening it with your breath, and especially breathe out very deeply, and sooner or later you will experience through your noise-removal process heat in your throat and upper chest near the end of each exhaled breath.

Experimentally noise-removal breathe in through different parts of your body. Feel a real pull as your breath comes in through those different areas, swirling up and carrying away the noise you are pushing out with your exhaled warm, rich breath.

Keep freeing your mind-brain-body-spirit system with this noise-removal breathing, feeling all kinds of stuff coming out. When you feel drained of all the noises in your body and mind, come fully alert, feeling terrifically good.

Now that you have established this experience of noise-removal breathing, you can turn the process on at any time, in any level of consciousness.

The Energy-Column Visualization*

Become very conscious of the top of your head.

Now also become very conscious of the bottoms of your feet.

Now become conscious of the space connecting the two, the top of your head and the bottoms of your feet.

Now, like filling up a transparent bottle with white milk, let that space fill and light up with tingling bright electric life energy.

Now extend one end of that column down through your feet,

* This is also from Win Wenger, creator of Psychegenics.

beyond the bottoms of your feet . . . extend that end of your energy column way down beyond the bottoms of your feet . . . *way* beyond.

Now extend the other end of that column way up through and beyond the top of your head—far—farther still—*way* farther still.

Now noise-removal breathe throughout this entire extended column of energy for five minutes or longer each time.

8

Replaying the Movies of Your Childhood

I inform the patient . . . that he will see before him a recollection.
And I pledge him to communicate this picture or idea to me.
—Sigmund Freud

I challenge you to remember the way things *really* were when you were growing up.

For a start, who was the boss in your house—your mother or your father? When they were together, *how* were they together? Did one lead the other . . . were they partners . . . or did they each have equal—but separate—powers?

With these questions in mind, you're ready to direct the following movie-of-the-mind.

Parents-Running-Through-a-Field Script

Begin by closing your eyes and letting yourself relax. Breathe deeply from your abdomen and feel the sweet relaxation that flows through your body.

Now, in your mind's eye, see a lovely green meadow in springtime. When you can sense it very clearly—the grass, the trees surrounding it, the wildflowers, perhaps even the butterflies and the sound of the breeze blowing through leaves—then see your mother and father running through this meadow.

Look at them closely and see the expressions on their faces and how their bodies move. Regardless of how far from real life the notion of them running in a field may be, let yourself go with the fantasy and watch them be there. Whether they look as they do today or as they did when you were a child makes no difference. The truth of the story is all that's important here.

As you watch them, ask yourself these questions. Are they both running or does one refuse to run? Who is running faster? Are they running very fast, at a medium pace, or dragging? What do their bodies look like as they run—stiff, relaxed, loose, tight? Take your time and just watch your movie unreel, noting everything that's happening.

This visualization lets you look at your parents in a new light, to see them in a way that may be very different from what you *believe* about them. You will probably find that your images of the way they run across a field are a parallel to the way they have moved through life. After you've done the exercise (and hopefully not before), here are some guidelines to help you interpret it.

It is more usual in our culture to see the father running faster than the mother as it is more likely that the man was dominant in the family. If the mother runs faster, it indicates that she may have been the dominant parent.

When their legs move freely and they're relaxed as they run, it is a sign of a relatively relaxed home environment. While there may have been areas of conflict in your childhood, they probably weren't shattering ones.

Those who have done this exercise and have a lot of conflict with their parents often report that the parents run stiffly; in fact, mental rigidity and rigid legs seem to go together, in life as in fantasy. When a parent tended to self-pity and martyrdom, he or she also usually had stiff limbs in the visualization.

A young woman who was having trouble getting away from

her mother's control told me that she saw her parents running in a brilliant golden field with large white clouds hovering overhead. They ran together up a long steep hill, her father running with his fists clenched; then her mother suddenly sprinted ahead, as though she were determined to win a race. As she told the story of her movie the young woman recognized how it paralleled her real situation. "My mother ran us all with her angry determination," she noted-bitterly. She fell silent for a moment and then began to cry. "I also see the most tremendous courage in her face."

That one session proved to be a breakthrough for her. She saw her mother as she really was, angry, determined—and also courageous. Putting her mother into perspective helped her to put herself into perspective. She now began to see that she could run her own life.

A patient of mine saw his mother begin by running alongside his father. Then, with no warning, she turned and ran in the opposite direction, upon which his father immediately followed. This triggered a flow of recollections which were very different from the way he had previously remembered his father. It also led to a new insight about his own marriage. Like his father, he was the pacifier in the marriage relationship, often at the expense of his feelings and deeper needs.

This particular technique is the creation of Akhter Ahsen, a Pakistani psychologist who came to the United States ten years ago with a theory he called "psycheye." I met Akhter soon after he arrived in Philadelphia, and began for the first time in my life to consider the value of pictures, rather than words, to reach the truth about a person's past. "Words are not experience," he told me then. "They merely talk about experience." Since that first meeting with Akhter, who has become one of the country's top experts in this field, my fascination with pictures of the mind has continued.

The parents-in-a-field visualization was one of those he used,

and the one I first used with myself. In creating my mother
and father running through a field, I saw my mother, who
had arthritis and walked awkwardly, pulling my father's arm
and almost dragging him through that field. It was enough
to convince me of the validity of Akhter's system. Although
I had chosen to deny it, my mother ran our household with
an iron hand!

Playing Detective in Your Childhood Home

Freud, the master himself, used visualization for a while
and then stopped in favor of other analytic tools. If he had
continued, the whole picture of psychotherapy during the past
fifty years might have been different.

What happens with many people who go into therapy is
that they simply repeat to the therapist the words they have
been repeating over and over again in their minds. Talking
about feelings is not the same as experiencing the feelings themselves. As a result, today there are many psychotherapists
working with pictures-in-the-mind, either as a primary therapy
technique or as an adjunct, to get their patients out of en-
trenched mind patterns about their childhoods.

When a patient replays the movies of his childhood, if only
for a few seconds, it actually catapults him out of old, often
paralyzing, thoughts into seeing the old situation in a brand-
new way. Bringing these old memories into consciousness has
the power to heal old wounds and bring people closer to
wholeness.

In my own practice I see repeatedly that, no matter how
miserable my patients may be, they cling to their distortions
about what may have happened when they were growing up.
The most effective way I've found to break through this is
to invite them to play detective in their own homes.

I suggest that they see themselves lying in bed as a child

and take in everything that's going on around them—the cracks in the ceiling, the feel of their bedspread, the smell of the house, the muffled sounds of their parents talking in another room.

After you've digested the experience of your parents running through a meadow, I suggest that you explore your own similar images from childhood. Not only can I promise that they'll be fascinating, you may also find a wonderful feeling of release in them.

A Script for Replaying Your Childhood

Pick any time or place in your life and see yourself there. When the movie begins to unreel, pay particular attention to the details of where you are. Really feeling yourself in that place sets the stage for the drama to unfold.

The most important things to notice during this movie are your thoughts and judgments. Be aware of them as they come—"I was right, he was wrong"; "I am bad, she was good"; "I never did anything right"; etc.—and then let them gently float out of your mind. Each one of these negative impulses simply reinforces old thoughts and prevents your movie from unreeling freely.

It is possible that you will see unhappy movies, and even fearful ones. Just as you would do when you watch a scary movie in a movie theater, simply watch it and feel whatever feelings it brings up, knowing that they will pass. When you are willing to look at the uncomfortable picture, it often changes to something happier by itself.

Dr. Robert Leichtman, a Baltimore psychiatrist who works with inner pictures, suggests that when you see a frightening figure—human or animal—on your private movie screen, you should offer it some food.

He tells the story of a patient who saw a huge bear appear

before her the moment after she had been visualizing her mother and father. She became frightened by the picture, and felt she might be crushed. When Dr. Leichtman suggested that she spread honey on the ground for the bear, her picture changed instantly, first to a panda, and then to a playful fox terrier.

At that instant she thought of her father, who had always frightened her. To her surprise, her next thought was of a man who needed love and tenderness. With that recognition her relationship with her father, which had always been guarded, began to change and she was able to feel her love for him. In return he let himself show the love for her that he had withheld out of fear of rejection. This lovely true story reminds us, again, that hidden behind our fears are often warmth, tenderness, and love. When people shut down what I call their "feeling systems," they cut themselves off from *all* emotion.

Dr. Peter Brill, a free-spirited psychiatrist at the University of Pennsylvania, shared with me this story in which he used movies-of-the-mind to help a man he worked with get in touch with his feelings.

Peter does "transition workshops" for men and women whose personal or career lives are in flux.

This particular person, a forty-five-year-old widower, simply could not express emotion; his face was humorless and dead-pan. He told Peter that his father had left his mother when he was three, and then died. He was brought up by his mother and grandmother, and said that he had always felt "frozen."

As part of the workshop program, the participants were instructed to think of a high or low moment in their childhoods and then to focus on whatever moment first came to their minds. The man remembered going to school for the first time, and his unbelievable fear. Then he suddenly remembered his Teddy bear, which he hadn't thought of in years.

At Peter's suggestion, he drew the Teddy bear on a large piece of child's construction paper. The memories then came rushing in. He remembered how his mother and grandmother had made fun of him for wanting the toy, and how humiliated he had felt. He specifically remembered that deeply upsetting moment when he put his Teddy bear in the closet for good. Through this replay of an important incident of his childhood, a flood of tears was released. He was then able to begin to connect with other feelings and to talk about them.

In explaining to me what happens in a case like this, Peter told me he believes that the important events in most of our lives are primarily visual experiences, and are retained in our memories as images. Like others who are now working with this remarkable tool, he has discovered that people get to these events much better through their stored inner images than by talking about them.

An Image Worth a Thousand Words

Psychosynthesis, created by Italian psychiatrist Dr. Roberto Assagioli (who died just a few years ago at the age of 84), is a most remarkable system using pictures in the mind's eye along with other techniques for psychotherapy, self-awareness, and growth.

An example of how this very effective system works can be seen through the true story of a woman who identified her main problem in life as a dominating husband. When she was asked to visualize the way she felt about the relationship, she immediately saw herself as a baby robin being held in someone's hand. The baby bird could not get away and was being crushed.

The therapist suggested that she see the hand opening. When she did, the bird flew away to a nearby branch, where it settled down and then refused to move. Try as she might to see the bird fly off the branch, it continued to hang on. From this image, she saw clearly that it was she who allowed herself to be dominated by her husband because it gave her a sense of security. And from this new recognition emerged another: that she alone was responsible for her situation and that she had the freedom to be dominated or not dominated as she chose. When she stopped blaming her husband for her predicament, she was able to see the other options in her life.

Robert Gerard, a Los Angeles psychotherapist who works with imagery, uses a visualization script he calls "the door."

The patient is asked to picture a door in a wall or at the entrance to a house and on the door imagine a word. That word can be suggested by the patient: anxiety, depression, love, hate, hope, for example. Then the patient opens the door and reports what he sees on the other side. In the spontaneous movie that follows, he will usually see an actual scene from childhood which is associated with the word—parents fighting, perhaps, or himself in a schoolroom being the target of ridicule.

What happens here is different from simply *remembering* a childhood incident which had been particularly upsetting, because the word on that door helps us to expand the way we now see the original event. We also see it more objectively than when we just remember, since remembering often has a possessive, holding-on quality about it.

For example, my brother had an amateur radio station, and I remember that he sometimes used to hold my fingers to the wires to give me a light electric shock (out of sight of my parents, naturally). Every time I thought back to that, I was filled with the original emotion of fear and anger. When I used Robert Gerard's technique and saw the word "fear" on that door, and then went through it to watch an incident when my brother gave me a shock, my images forced me to let go of what I remembered. For the first time, I saw the fear in *my brother's* eyes while he was doing it, which was an incredible revelation for me. I then looked at myself and saw clearly that I had invited his attack by my teasing and defiance. Bringing my memory in line with the truth, I could never again blithely recite the lines, "When I was a little girl, my brother used to grab my hands and give me an electric shock with wires." It was a story that had once served me wonderfully when I saw myself as a victim, but which now I could accept as only a fraction of the truth.

A Script for Getting to the Truth

Right at this moment, surely, you have an old or current anger or resentment which runs through your mind. Either it continually preoccupies you, or it pops up just at the moment when you want nothing more than to have a good night's rest. To help yourself move through and let go of it, try this:

Picture the word that is most applicable to the problem you now have, and see it clearly in huge block letters marked on a door. Pick the door carefully and note the details of it. Perhaps it is an ornately carved antique door or it is a very simple wooden or painted door. Now see the word you've chosen standing out clearly on that door.

Very gently open that door and look in front of you, to the left and to the right to see what is there, just as you would if you went into a room you had never been in before.

If you see a person, begin to talk with that person about your problem. If you see nothing but a vast horizon, continue on and see another door, and go through that one until you can find a person or an animal with whom you can talk about your problem or a place where you can be alone with it.

Give yourself time to be with the problem. Then give yourself time to see what the truth about the situation is. Old memories and people associated with them may come onto your screen.

See how they relate to it. See them as they *are,* even if it's different from the way you *think* they are.

Now open your eyes and put your left-brain to work by deliberately figuring out what the images are saying to you. You can now take those insights into your life and put them to work for you. What they've told you is what you need to know.)

What Do You Believe Right Now?

As you've replayed some of the movies of your childhood, you've discovered that a lot of what you *thought* was true either *never* was true or *no longer* is true. You've also discovered that you had to go beyond thoughts and memories about the past to find what the reality actually was.

Can you do that for something that concerns you right now? Can you consider *a way to know* that goes beyond your intellectual arsenal . . . beyond "proven" truths . . . beyond the answers that served you five years ago? Can you, instead, close your eyes, send your concerns into the core of your being, and then consider what emerges as the most important thing you need to know?

Only you know what's true for you. And only by going beneath what you *believe* to be true, and being willing to *experience* what's true for you at the moment, can you really *know* what the truth is.

An architect, Donald Kenneth Busch, helps interior designers and others who are creating living environments to go beyond what's currently fashionable (which usually determines their taste) to discover what *they* really like. He does this by using movies-of-the-mind to guide them to their childhood homes, where they explore in detail the textures, colors, patterns, and shapes in all the rooms. "People find out things

they would really like in their environment now, that they
had as kids," Busch says. "They rediscover colors and other
things that are important to them, like a sense of space if
they were room-sharers or lived in railroad flats, or textures
and lighting that they really like but had rejected when they
were decorating their homes." He concedes that this can be
an expensive adventure. Many of his clients want to immediately redecorate their homes!

We all run our lives on what we *believe*. Whether these
beliefs are conscious or not makes little difference (although
the unconscious beliefs have more power than the conscious
ones because they aren't available to us to be challenged).
Their existence prevents us from experiencing life spontaneously.

To get a sense of what *you* believe, try asking yourself these
questions:

What do I need to be happy? Remembering the last time
I felt happy, what was it that made me feel that way? When
I think right now of something in my life that I feel happy
about, what comes to mind? How are the answers to the three
questions different and how are they alike?

What makes a person or an object beautiful? What is the
most beautiful thing in my life right at this moment? What
are the qualities about the latter that are different from the
answer to the first question?

How does my stomach feel when I feel healthy? My head?
The back of my neck? My knees? How do I feel right now?
When I now close my eyes and go in my mind's eye to each
of these places, how do they feel? Do they feel the same or
different from the way I believed they would feel?

Most of our beliefs are disconnected from what we feel and
sense and know at any particular moment. They are attitudes
we have absorbed and then made part of an automatic system
that acts as predictably as a machine when its "on" button

is pushed. Since our beliefs trigger everything that happens in our lives, in the same way a sophisticated machine's "on" button triggers a predictable set of events, *what we believe is what we get.*

The man who goes through life convinced that he's a failure, *guarantees* his failure.

The woman who *believes* she'll always be fat, always *is* fat.

The child who's certain his brother is smarter, always manages to prove it with his school reports.

The young couple who believe that love conquers all thrive in the face of all their difficulties. And so it goes.

To begin to see the connection between your beliefs and what happens in your life, you need to begin finding out what it is that you believe. And then to compare what you believe with what your actual experience is—what you know. Your movies-of-the-mind are the most important tool you have for this.

"Blowing Your Mind" to Get to Know Yourself

The process that can produce clear and accurate pictures of your childhood home and the solution to your most immediate problem, and tell you what you and you alone know to be true, does this by literally "blowing the mind"—bypassing it and leaving it momentarily speechless. In going beyond the mind you will find a far wiser, more reliable, and more sensitive source of knowing than is possible in any other way.

That source is your inner self. It is the part of you that is more than your thoughts or feelings or memories. It is who you really are. And the best way to get to know it is to use it. For a start, here are some ways to discover—and rediscover—yourself.

Tap your memories, as you've begun to do already, to discover the buried images from your past that continue to control you and keep you from being truly alive at this moment. (You might discover, as I did just recently, that a grudge against my brother experienced in childhood and carried into adulthood was a total distortion of those moments long ago.)

Explore your body to get to know it inside and out, to discover where it feels strong and where it is weak, to reexamine your belief about a particular part of you that you don't like, to find and relieve the areas of tension.

Find out what you're really feeling. Are you sitting on a geyser of anger? Does your feeling of easiness actually mask a state of numbness protecting you from pain? Do you feel "lousy" because something has upset you, or because you don't really know what it's like to feel good? Do you feel wonderful, in which case can you enjoy it?

Discover your beauty. For most of us, it's just as hard to see and accept our strengths and our positive qualities as it is to acknowledge that which we hate about ourselves. Robert Burns wrote wistfully of seeing ourselves as others see us. Our inner movies can let us do just that if we choose to use them in that way. In reflecting back to ourselves the best and the worst in us, we can use this priceless information to guide all our actions.

Dare to ask yourself "Who Am I?" and expect a response that will be deeply satisfying. Dr. Roberto Assagioli has said: "You can trust your deepest being and learn to live from that place. The real you knows all that you need to know, knows the future, will lead you." Dr. Assagioli, as have many others who have followed him, saw visualization as the channel to the higher self—the essential core of one's being, the spark of one's uniqueness, the connection to all of life—which is the source of both our individuality and our universality. It is from this place that life takes on the richness, the meaning, and the pleasure that most of us long for.

9

Expanding Your Mind to Reach Your Creative Imagination

> Every second we live is a new and unique moment of the universe, a moment that never was before and will never be again. And what do we teach our children in school? We teach them that two and two make four and that Paris is the capital of France. We should say to each of them, "Do you know what you are? You are a marvel. You are unique. In the millions of years that have passed, there has never been another child like you."
>
> —Pablo Casals

I let my body sink into the carpet beneath me, closed my eyes, and in the soothing darkness yielded to . . . experiencing an apple.

I saw the apple in its myriad details: its illusion of smoothness giving way to a glossy landscape of diverse and unexpected surprises; the cleavage from which its stem grew holding the mystery of unexplored delights; its redness a palette of infinite shades and hues in ever-changing combinations.

Then my sense of smell joined my visual adventure, bringing to my experience the ecstasy of sweet, ripe perfume of apple. My taste buds quivered in anticipation of being touched by its tangy, crunchy appleness. And my stomach gurgled in response to the memory of gentle tartness. For a few minutes the ecstasy of the imagined experience joined with the pleasure of a real experience of an apple when one was placed in my hand. I explored it with my fingers, my taste buds, my ears, my eyes.

Then I went back to the experience of my mind's eye and suddenly *became* an apple. I was a beautiful apple on an apple tree in an exquisite apple orchard, and I felt the warm sun on my skin and a soft breeze blowing my leaves as I luxuriated in my appleness.

As an apple I then regressed in time, becoming a smaller, greener, tarter apple, and then an apple blossom. I heard the honey bees buzzing around me and a farmer's dog barking in the distance. I felt my relationship to the sun, the earth, the air, the insects, and the seasons—and it felt wonderful.

I then became the whole apple tree on which I, as an apple, was growing. With my roots I felt myself reaching into the dark, damp soil and smelled its fertile fragrance. I reached out for life-giving water and nutrients and, lo, became the water itself in the damp orchard field. I felt myself feeding the grasses and wild flowers. I felt myself part of the larger unity of nature. My experience went on and on—feeling myself form into a soft cloud, becoming a raindrop, becoming an apple again on a rainy day and, finally, returning to the here-and-now.

I opened my eyes to find myself in a geodesic dome, lying like a spoke in a wheel (with a dozen or so other participants providing the other spokes) on a blue-carpeted platform, and suddenly remembering where I was and what I was there for.

Where I was was in the Imaginarium, created at Stanford University by the brilliant direction of Robert McKim. What I was doing there was seeking an understanding of the relationship between visual thinking and creativity. And what I had discovered was still another link in a chain that led inevitably to the inner self as the source of our most valuable responses to life. Here, too, the focus was on tapping the vast unmined riches of the mind's eye.

McKim is among a new breed of thinkers drawn from the fields of engineering, education, psychology, and science who are exploring the effects of imagination on our development as healthy and creative people. Professor of design engineering at Stanford University, McKim's title only hints at the breadth of his interests and work there.

Concerned with finding ways to expand his students' thinking about design problems, McKim's experiments led him to design his own version of a geodesic dome and put it in the corner of a high-ceilinged university classroom. It was to serve as a special environment where people could get away from noise and other distractions to explore their inner images. He called it, appropriately, the Imaginarium.

Sitting under a tree on the sunny, rolling campus at Stanford, McKim talked about his creation with me. "By looking at pictures in the mind's eye," he told me, "we can get a brand new way of seeing a problem." He went on to say that the dome was designed to allow people to discover the imaginative activity that *already* exists in them. He feels that his methods unblock—rather than enhance—what is already there. The person who can use his or her imagination flexibly, he explained, sees creatively. The person who can't budge his or her imagination to see other viewpoints, on the other hand, experiences only a one-sided view of reality.

The construction of the Imaginarium was intended as a physical duplication of the inner sensory world. The "mind's eye" is recreated by a spherical optical lens and equipment which projects images onto the dome's entire visual field. The "mind's ear" is the sophisticated sound system which fills the auditory consciousness with sounds and music. In addition, the sound system is connected to speaker coils attached underneath the platform. Switched on, the coils vibrate the platform, allowing the sound to be experienced tactilely. To round out the sensory input, scents can be introduced into the dome through the air-conditioning system. (What fun it was to smell an apple this way!)

In the unique environment of the Imaginarium it becomes both possible and easy to become an apple, as I had done, or take a cosmic trip to the end of the universe and then zoom backward into the nucleus of an atom (another Imaginarium program) all through movies-of-the-mind. At the end, we confront the last remaining barrier we might have to using our inner senses—the idea so many of us hold that movies-of-the-mind are irrational or useless—by sharing our experience. For each one of us it has been literally mind-boggling and the sharing releases our awe and excitement with our new discovery.

How to Tap Your Own Creative Imagination

Contrary to what most of us believe, *the ability to develop creative ideas can be learned and expanded at any stage in our lives.*

How do we do this?

First of all, we know that the creative person is someone who is ready to abandon old classifications and to accept that life is rich with new possibilities. He or she is willing to continually challenge his or her belief systems and explore new ways of looking.

We know, also, that the extent of a person's imagination reflects an ability to visualize something that has neither been seen nor experienced before. Creativity tends to come in the form of pictures, not as ideas in the form of words.

We know that the creative process itself involves, first, a certain amount of input or preparation from the mind, which is then followed by a period of germination, which in turn gives birth to an insight or inspiration or creative flash. This sudden "knowing" almost invariably comes as an image, either symbolic or realistic.

Some Things to Keep in the Outer Mind About Using the Inner Mind

To bring forth creative inspiration, there are certain things you should keep in mind. Some of this you already know and some of it may be new to you. It is summarized here to allow you to return to it whenever you need a reminder.

1. The creative response happens in a state of relaxed attention. It is in this state that we have access to our images and are free from continued censorship and old beliefs.

You can reach this state with one of the relaxations suggested in this book, or with one you already know or from another source. The creative response can also occur in other relaxed situations—taking a walk, waking up from a nap, jogging, daydreaming, for example. Mozart's ideas often came while riding in a carriage or walking after a good meal; Samuel Johnson spoke of needing a purring cat when he wrote; Henri Poincaré discovered a breakthrough in mathematics while walking on a beach.

2. The *active* part of the creative process is to do the *homework,* or *study,* or *discipline* that requires the use of the will and intellect. If you're a composer that might mean learning how to play a number of instruments to understand how they work. If you're a scientist, that might mean reviewing the available data and then designing a research program to prove or disprove your thesis.

3. The *receptive* part of the creative process is a *waiting* and *tuning in. We must consciously want the response and then be willing to wait for it.* This is a time of germination, or incubation, when trying to get results becomes self-defeating.

4. The *creative response* comes as an *inspiration,* or *insight,*

or *flash*—often when we least expect it. It comes in the state of relaxed attention which we mentioned earlier. Robert McKim calls this "the paradox of ho-hum and aha!" We can make room for it to happen in a receptive visualization. When we do this, we deliberately put ourselves in a situation in which we can become aware of our movies-of-the mind.

5. Immediately *write down the insight images* or *talk about them* as soon as they come to you. The images that emerge spontaneously from the inner self are fleeting and easily forgotten, as we know from our experience with dreams. When we "capture" the material from the unconscious, we can then look at it and work with it. In that way we bring the artist and the scientist within each of us together. The activity of writing or speaking also keeps us grounded in reality.

6. And, finally, *put your inspirations and insights to work for you*. That's what they're there for. You betray your creative process if you don't use it, act on it, and share it with others.

An important part of this process is learning to recognize the creative response when it comes. It may come in a shorthand form, with one image or symbol or word expressing a complicated concept. It may also come accompanied by a sense of rightness, an "aha," with feelings of excitement and release to tell you that you've found what you went looking for. Follow your feelings rather than your intellect. You can check them later against what you already know.

The Role of Imagination in Children

How many times have you heard parents or teachers say: "Stop daydreaming and find something to do" or "Don't just sit there staring into space; get to work" or "Make up another story like that one and you'll spend the rest of the day in your room" or, when a child plays with an imaginary friend, "I wish you'd find somebody *real* to play with"?

The rejection of imagination in favor of what we call "the real world" is so deeply ingrained in our culture that our children's creative spirit has all but been squashed in the name of education. We believe that putting all our efforts into developing left-brain functions—reading, writing, and arithmetic, for a start—is what will make our kids successful, and therefore happy. We assume, of course, that success and happiness have to do mostly with achievement and the material benefits which it often brings.

Our educational system tends to look at right-brain functions—imagination, intuition, visualization—as a kind of regressed or primitive way of thinking. Except in the arts, which get woefully little attention, the richness available to the inner eye is ignored while we conscientiously master facts, memorize, and learn by rote. After 11,000 hours in the classroom, which is about what we've put in by the time we finish high school, and almost as much time spent watching television, presumably we're ready to make our way in the world. But by that time our inner consciousness is almost totally shut down and with it the creativity we need to continually deal with the problems and meet the challenges in our lives. Small wonder that leaders in business and education are labeling our young people dull conformists and lamenting their lack of imagination.

We're only now beginning to see the cost of this lopsided value system—and what we've been denied through it.

We're finding, for example, that the qualities that reap rewards of wealth, responsibility, or prestige are mainly right-brain functions: originality, flexibility of thought, and sensitivity.

A psychologist who has done extensive research on imagination (and the lack of it) in children confirms this in his own findings. Yale University's Dr. Jerome Singer says that children's ability to make-believe helps them more sharply to distinguish between what's real and what's fantasy. The more they develop their imagination, Dr. Singer has discovered, the richer their lives can be expected to be. "Pretending and make-believe are very special qualities of human experience," he says, "because they provide us with a sense of our mysterious and powerful capacities. . . . Through our ability to imagine things we can indeed transcend time and space in a remarkable fashion."

Movies-of-the-Mind in the Classroom

A teacher in Sacramento, California, is expanding her students' creative imagination through science, and vice versa, using movies-of-the-mind. Marjorie King is one of the new breed of teachers who are concerned with developing the right-brain along with the more traditional education of the left-brain. She does this by using guided imagery to help her students understand the subjects they're studying in science. In a class where they were exploring the mechanics of breathing, for example, she suggested that they each imagine themselves an oxygen atom and then take a trip into their bodies. Here is one student's report of the experience.

I got on an oxygen atom and went into my lungs and saw how black they were. Then I went into a blood vessel that looked like a highway and went to the heart and when I went in it, it looked like a door opened up. I went inside and it looked like a freeway in L.A. Then I went back out and the door opened to let me out.

When I got out it looked like a big, big highway, then I went to go to my finger. On the way to it the highway got smaller and smaller. Then my friend [the oxygen atom] and I got to a cave which was too small for us and my four-speed red sports car, so we got off it and went through the cave and went into a cell and in there there was a big factory and lightning all over the cell. Then I went out of the cell back into the blood. But my sports car was blue this time and not red, and I'd picked up a hitchhiker [a carbon dioxide atom] and went on to the heart again. The door opened up and we went through it and out of it down to the lungs and out with my new friend.

What an incredible adventure, as remarkable for its biological accuracy as for its intrinsic drama. It is not likely that this student, a so-called "problem learner," will easily forget the essentials of respiration.

Jack Canfield, who heads the Institute for Humanistic and Transpersonal Education in Boston, an organization devoted to expanding children's experience in the classroom, sees the use of imagination as the door to all the creative energies within us. In his work with children and teen-agers, he uses movies-of-the-mind to help them become aware of themselves as well as for problem-solving. Images, he says, have knowledge. It is this knowledge that he helps them discover.

As an example of the way he works, he told me how he reached an eight-year-old through movies-of-the-mind. Jack began by telling the boy to pretend that he was a motorcycle and then to find out if he was a rusty one or a brand-new one and whether he moved fast or slow. The little boy was delighted with the idea. He closed his eyes and reported that he was a slow-moving, rusty, and kind of worn-out motorcycle. Jack then suggested that he change the picture in his mind to see himself as a shiny, new, and speedy motorcycle, which the youngster was able to do. When he had first come in that day he had literally been dragging his feet. After he saw himself as shiny and new, he became much livelier and moved more quickly.

The way Jack might use this in the classroom is to have the children visualize a subject and then show them a film about it so they can test their own experience against outer reality. He told me about one group of children who were studying the colonization of bees. They were asked to close their eyes and each become a bee, flying back and forth to the hive, feeling what it was like to live with other bees. By the time the movie was shown, their interest was very high. It was amazing, he told me, how similar their own experience was to what they later saw on film. By combining the inner and outer experience here, the right- and left-brain functions were merged for a much more powerful learning experience.

The Inner Mind Sharpens the Outer Mind

Dr. Gerald Jampolsky has a particular interest in learning problems, stemming from his own reading problems as a child. His teachers, he told me, used to blame the "ants in his pants" for the fact that he didn't seem to be "trying hard enough." He was trying as hard as he could, but he was slow to develop the skills needed for reading. Not until medical school, where he found one of his strongest areas to be clinical medicine, were his other skills and talents considered equally important to his education.

Jerry is a spare, handsome psychiatrist in his early fifties, whose personal warmth is echoed in his office, a cozy, sun-filled, book-lined room overlooking the San Francisco Bay. One of his most fascinating ventures (you've already read about several of them earlier in these pages) was a program he developed for a group of third- and fourth-grade children who were having trouble learning to read. His goal was to teach the children to relax and then offer them a new way of learning through feeling and inner seeing.

He began his work with them by having them imagine certain sensations: the feeling of fur on the face, a weight pulling the arm down, a balloon pulling the arm up. Since these children initially had poor visual memory, recalling feelings was a first step toward recalling pictures. One of the visualizations he then used was to have them put their hands on their heads, mentally open up their skulls, lift their brains out, and then with a hose, wash off all the dirt and grime that kept them from learning. When they returned their brains to their heads, they felt freer and lighter. While they were doing this, they were encouraged to get rid of their old belief system and replace it with a new one that believes that anything is possible and nothing is impossible.

The children went on to imagine themselves writing a short book on their favorite subject. Then they visualized themselves reading their own books fluently, successfully, and happily. Taking this mental picture of themselves reading, they then put it into the blood cells which would go to all the tissues of the body, including the brain. The children were instructed to do this five to ten minutes each night and again before going to school in the morning.

At the same time he was working with the children, Jerry had contact with their parents and teachers. They, too, were shown how to use movies-of-the-mind and then were asked to see their children reading successfully and without effort. Because of the impact of their unspoken thoughts, they were also asked to mentally stop criticizing the children.

Incredibly, in one month's time the average reading skill of these children increased by one-and-a-half years. Along with this remarkable accomplishment, parents and teachers also observed that their children had more self-esteem and seemed more content than before they began the program.

Mind-Stretching Scripts

Here, I suggest three scripts to help you develop your own special powers of imagination. They have been designed to open the door to creative activity that is ongoing and pervasive. Each of them can be expanded in innumerable ways, limited only—not surprisingly—by your imagination!

One suggestion: totally accept whatever comes up for you or others who might play these games with you. All our inner experiences are real and true. There is no right or wrong, or good or bad, or healthy or neurotic way to do this. Whatever you see inside you is as valid as what you see in any other way.

Exercising Your Inner Eye*

Taking your time, translate each of the following descriptions into a mental image. Go back and do it again in a few weeks and then a few weeks later, and notice the difference. Notice the difference, also, in the way you see things—inner as well as outer—after you've done these exercises.

Now sense (see, smell, taste, feel, or hear) with your mind's eye:

- a familiar face
- a galloping horse
- a rosebud
- your bedroom
- a changing stoplight
- a newspaper headline
- the sound of rain on the roof
    the voice of a friend
    children laughing at play
- the feel of soft fur
    an itch
    a gentle breeze on your face
- the muscular feeling of running
    of kicking a can
    of drawing a circle on paper

* This is adapted from imagery suggested in Robert H. McKim's *Experiences in Visual Thinking*.

- the taste of a lemon
  of toothpaste
  of a potato chip
- the smell of bacon frying
  of a gardenia
  of perspiration
- the feeling of hunger
  of a cough
  of coming awake
- a stone dropped into a quiet pond with concentric ripples
  forming and expanding outward
- this book flying away, high into the blue sky, finally disappearing
- your shoe coming apart in slow motion and each piece
  drifting away into space
- an orange being cut into five equal pieces and the pieces
  being arranged in three different patterns

A Game Called All Over*

This game is read aloud to one or more participants. The
reader should pause after each slash (/) to give the listeners
a chance to form the fantasy. A sensitive reading pace can
be established by having the listener signal when they're ready
to go on (a raised finger, a grunt, etc.).

Fill your head full of water./ Have the water spray out of
your ears./ Have it spray out of your nose./ Have it spray
out of your eyes./ Have it spray out of your mouth./ Have
the water go back into your ears./ Have it go back into your
nose./ Have it go back into your eyes./ Have it go back into
your mouth./ Have it spray out of all those places again./ Have
it go in again./ What do you want it to do now?/ All right.

* From Richard De Mille's *Put Your Mother on the Ceiling.*

Have a fire in your stomach./   Have your stomach full of ice./ Have it full of hot cereal./   Have it full of water./   Have it full of nothing./   Have it full of ice cream./   Have it full of sand./ Have nothing in it at all./   Have no stomach./   Have a new stomach./   What do you want to do about your stomach now?/ All right.

Have your backbone get hot./   Have it get cold./   Have it get soft./   Have it get hard./   Have it turn blue./   Have it turn white./   Have it turn any color you like./   Take it out and throw it away./   Have a new backbone./   Have it crooked./   Have it straight./   Take it out./   Tie it in a bow./   Throw it away./ Have a new one./   Have it come apart and fall on the floor in pieces./   Have a new backbone./   What do you want to do with it?/   All right.

Have your skin be cold./   Have it be hot./   Have it turn blue./ Have it turn green./   Have it turn to wood./   Have it get furry./ Have it grow scales like a fish./   Have it grow feathers./ Have it get smooth./   Have it be beautiful./   Have it get sores all over./   Have it be smooth again./   Have it feel good./   Have it itch./   Have it burning with fire all over./   Have it all burn up./   Have a new skin./   Have it soft and smooth./   Have it tough as leather./   Have it hard as rock./   Have it soft and smooth./   How do you want it now?/   All right.

Brainstorm an Idea

Brainstorming has traditionally been done verbally. Here you will brainstorm an idea in your inner eye (or ear if it is something musical, or taste buds if it is something to cook or eat).

1. Pick a concept or a problem or a challenge that intrigues you. You might want to pick several, sleep on them, and then decide on the one you like best.

2. Breathe deeply and go to a place on your inner screen that's peaceful and lovely. Then put the brainstorming subject on your inner screen.

3. Tell yourself you want to explore all the possibilities and then watch them come. They may come in groups, followed by a period of quiet, and then come in groups again. Do not judge what comes up as terrific or awful or anything in-between.

4. In a notebook or on a sketch pad, quickly note down every image or idea. Set a quantity goal for a certain period of time— say two or three dozen in an hour. Whatever comes up, however unimportant it may seem, note it down.

5. At the end of the time period, look over what you've done. Note how rich and diverse your imagination is.

6. Feel good knowing you have a wonderful imagination and that you have the power to make it even more so.

10

Love, Sex, Friendship (and Other Relationships) in a New Dimension

> Every person and all the events in your life are there because you have drawn them there. What you choose to do with them is up to you.
>
> —Richard Bach, *Illusions: The Adventures of a Reluctant Messiah*

I spent an afternoon watching Dr. Gerald Jampolsky lead a workshop of nurses and other medical personnel who work with very sick children. His objective was to help them to work with the children's own healing powers. He saw the basic issue as one of communication. He approached it by guiding them to their hearts through the mind's eye.

After a group relaxation exercise, in which they all closed their eyes and were guided to a deep inner place, he began the visualization by suggesting that each of the participants choose an age between four and seventeen and imagine being that age. "See yourself as perfectly healthy," he instructed them. "Then, suddenly, one day you begin to have a pain in your stomach. You feel weak." He paused after each image to allow people to see and feel the state he had described. "Your doctor examines you and takes samples for laboratory tests. Finally the results come through. The doctor tells you that you have leukemia or perhaps another type of cancer. He tells you that it's possible that you might die."

The instructions hung in the air while the group took them in. I saw people flinch, wrap their arms around themselves, wipe away the tears forming in the corners of their eyes. The experience was very real.

Jerry then led the group through the feelings, and especially the feeling of fear, of being sick with a fatal disease. "Ask yourself, 'Why me?'" he told them. "Then deny that fear, like it is a bad dream. How do you do it? What kinds of things are you going to do to hide your fear?"

He then guided the group to another situation. They were still children, and now they were riding on their bicycles to school or to a friend's house. "Suddenly, from out of nowhere, a truck is there. It slams into your bike. You go unconscious." A long pause here. "For eighty-two days you remain in a coma. No one is sure if you will live, die, or become a living vegetable. You wake up after eighty-two days to find that you are paralyzed. Now," he again paused, "allow yourself to experience the fear and the confusion that overwhelm you."

I saw by their body responses that they were very much there. They were uncomfortable, sad, frightened. But there was more. "Now imagine," Jerry continued, "all the things you have to go through now, which you all know so well. In and out of hospitals, clinics, doctors' offices. All the tests and needles and pills and EEG's. The bone-marrow explorations. Above all, the uncertainty. The not knowing if you will ever be whole again. Allow yourself to be in the hospital and to feel the fear and isolation of those long, lonely nights.

"Who can you talk to about how you really feel?" he asks. "What can you do about the feelings of wanting to rip that needle from your arm, run out of the hospital, and run home to where everything is exactly the way it used to be? Where can you find someone who cares about you and can help you through these agonizing moments?"

The impact of these questions was profound. As Jerry gently

brought the group back to the here and now, they looked young and vulnerable. In the few moments they had spent in their inner spaces they *became* the children they work with. For the first time, they really knew what it was like to be a sick child who might be dying. In discussing the experience afterward, they all agreed that they had had no conception of what it could be like. Some of them admitted to not ever having wanted to know. Listening to them, I had no doubt that this small event had unalterably affected the way they would now practice their professions.

This is a very new way for many of us to look at communications among and between people. At its root is the belief that to really relate to another person we need to really know what that person's feelings and experiences are. We use the power of movies-of-the-mind because it takes us way beyond what we can know with our senses and conscious minds, and lets us tune in at another level. *When we let go of our egos, with their investment in being right and better—and thus isolated, we dissolve the barriers that separate us from others. We can then yield to fully "being" with another human being.*

Becoming the Other Person

Through movies-of-the-mind we can actually experience the essence of another person by *becoming*, through the mind's eye, that other person (see, especially, the script on p. 136). We can know their truth as well as we know our own.

To write this ability off as ESP, with the ambivalence that evokes in people, is to do ourselves a great injustice. We have all experienced knowing the thoughts and feelings of a person we're very close to. In a receptive state, through relaxation techniques or meditation, we contact a much more profound knowing. It is as though we were each a deep well; in going to the bottom of our individual wells we ultimately come to an underground stream that is the source of all the wells. It is at that level that the barriers that keep us from knowing each other as ourselves dissolve.

We can use the power of visualization to transcend our separateness in many different ways.

In a close relationship, movies-of-the-mind allows us to know other people beyond what can be known at a verbal and physical level. We experience them as they really are: their real sorrows, needs, worries, longings, wishes, joys.

I have been very moved by the way I've seen this tool used by couples. When they've communicated with each other at a level beyond words and senses, they can feel in perfect harmony because they have become fully aware and accepting of each other at the moment. Most of us relate to those we love by seeing them as we want them to be. We have unconscious expectations and demands of them, and these cause havoc in the relationship. If we allow ourselves to know what *is,* and let go of the fantasies that keep us from accepting that, then we can love in a very fulfilling way. Werner Erhard sums it up perfectly: *"Loving another person is giving them the 'space' to be who they are, and who they are not."*

Tuning in to Someone Else

In Chapter 3 we met Bill, the assistant dean of a large university, who used this very technique to create a new way of relating to his boss. In his visualization, he saw his colleague as vulnerable and frightened, as opposed to Bill's conscious image of him as powerful and tough. As is not unusual in this process, he had a clairvoyant experience in which he saw that his boss had just learned that he had a serious medical problem. He also saw the effect of his own behavior, which was dramatically different from what he had assumed.

The imagery that led Bill to this, and which you can use

or vary for yourself, began with picturing his office. He saw where the desks and other furniture were and which doors were open and which shut. Then he went to the office of the person with whom he felt most in conflict. He saw that person at his desk working. He watched his eyes and noticed the way his body moved. He tuned into his thoughts.

Then he observed himself walking into that person's office and sitting in the chair he wanted to sit in. He looked at the other person directly in the eyes and said whatever it was he had been wanting to say for a month or a year or maybe ten years. Then he waited for an answer. In this experience he understood levels of the relationship that he had never perceived before. And he found it (as you will also) very liberating.

You can do this to "visit" anyone—a parent, a friend, a colleague. In a state of relaxation, simply allow yourself in your mind's eye to be with him or her. You can ask direct questions and you can enter into a dialogue with that person. What's essential here is to allow whatever comes up to just *be*. You might be surprised and hear something positive when you expected a negative, or vice versa. Take it in—and know that you've been in touch with reality, although a different reality than you're probably used to.

One couple I work with seek—and find—solutions to their problems this way. First they go deeply into themselves to find an answer or direction. Then they project themselves into the mind and body of the other person and experience both the problem and the possible solutions through the other's experience. It is very effective, especially for resolving difficulties that come up between them.

Another couple used this approach to deal with a sexual problem. Through their mind's eye they allowed themselves to enter the other person's body and be that other person. Then they saw and felt what it was like to make love as the other person, and to feel the sexual tension and release. Because they were reluctant to discuss the problem with each other, initially they did the visualization apart from each other and without sharing it. Sometime later, they did it a second time together.

Great clarity for both of them came out of these visualizations. They each had a deep misconception about what it was like to be the other in a sexual situation. When they saw themselves from a different perspective, free from their "beliefs" about the male or female sexual experience, they discovered that their responses were far more alike than different. In some way, they had both felt "used" by each other before. They were now able to take the first step toward the mutual pleasure of their lovemaking.

We all have the ability to project ourselves into the consciousness of another person, regardless of how near or far they are, or the nature of the relationship. And we can ask them questions—and get answers. In the course of my own visualizations, I learned that a former lover very adamantly had no interest in getting together again; that one of my children, whom I hadn't been in touch with for a week, had a bad cold; and that a dear friend of mine, who was in a crisis, was greatly helped by what I had conveyed to her in a movie-of-the-mind.

This power is in all of us. Right now, at this very moment, you can experience this wonderful aspect of yourself.

A Script for Knowing Someone in a New Way

This script can be used with two or more people experiencing each other at the same time or it can be done alone, with the visualizer focusing on someone not physically in the same room.

It can be used to "get into" someone you're deeply involved

with. Or to role-play another person (such as a man if you're a woman, or vice versa). Or to know in a different way a co-worker, a parent, a friend, or someone you just want to get to know better. Or it can be used to understand the experience of someone you respect and admire, as a prototype or inspiration for your own growth, perhaps a public figure or a great philosopher.

To help you focus on each of the directions, you might want to have someone read them to you. Or, if you want, you can read them slowly onto a tape to play back to yourself. Pause after each suggestion to allow time to explore the images that come up.

Begin by relaxing your body and breathing deeply from the abdomen. (A leisurely relaxation exercise is appropriate here.)

Go in your mind's eye to a very beautiful place where you have felt relaxed and peaceful.

Bring the person who you want to get to know in this visualization to this special place. Look at him or her very closely. Notice the face: the eyes, the nose, the mouth, the shape, the expression. Then look at that person's body. See the way that person is when quiet and when in motion. What does the way the body is held convey to you?

Begin to consider what it would be like to be the person you are with. What it would be like to be in the body you are observing. How it would feel to be in that whole mind-body system.

Go *into* that body now so that it is you in that body. Feel that your new body increasingly gives you the identity of that person who a few moments ago was separate from you.

Touch whatever you are seated on, knowing how *this* body touches things. Feel through your fingers and hands what these new sensations feel like. How are they different from what you're used to? How are they the same?

Now take on all *this* body's perceptions, looking out at the world through *these* eyes. Look at that person who *was* yourself, and from this new perspective, take in the person who used to be yourself.

On your inner screen, now get up and move around, experiencing the consciousness that goes with the movements of this new body.

Now examine the sensory possibilities of being that other person. Touch a beautiful object and feel how it feels. Taste a delicious food and experience what it's like to have that food come into your body. Listen to music or the sound of the woods or waves crashing on the beach. Is it different from the way you might experience these things in your own body?

Being this person, how do you feel about the world around you? Are you more or less happy than you were as yourself? Are you more or less wise? Are you more or less fearful than you were before? Are you more or less angry? More or less loving? And are you more or less alive, feeling what it's like to be this other person?

Perhaps there is something important that you want to know as this other person. Ask yourself whatever it is. Ask yourself how you feel about this particular thing you want to know about.

Now, slowly, find yourself moving back into the body that normally is yours. Your consciousness shifts back into that body, and this transference is easy, fast, complete. You are now that body, that person, that you were before.

And now open your eyes and be in the present, in your own self, and enjoy the feel of being yourself again.

How To Create a Relationship

We've been talking up to now about how to use *receptive visualization* to relate to another person.

With *programmed visualization,* you use the power of your mind to actually *create* what it is you want in a relationship.

You do this by seeing in your mind's eye the person or the situation exactly as you would have it be.

How can you use this process?

The most wonderful way to use it is to create a person for you to love. Visualizing the man or woman you want to be with is a very powerful creative force. It could, and ideally should, cover all the things you feel you really need and want.

Margot shared the following story with me. The man she created in her mind's eye was tall, in his forties, and attractive. She sensed (rather than actually saw) herself and this man making very deep connections—intellectually, emotionally, sexually, and spiritually. She experienced herself finding him both very attractive and very sexy. (She later added to her visualization the sense of him being potent, after being with men who weren't!) She saw him as well-established professionally and as being comfortable with her own success and assertiveness. He also had a softness and sweetness about him, she told me, which she had sorely missed in most of the men she had known. And, finally, two very important qualities: a sense of humor and *joie de vivre,* and an affection for children—especially hers.

While she visualized she also experienced what such a relationship would feel like. She told me that she often felt the warm, yielding feeling of giving over to another person in love. She also felt the excitement that this man stirred in her—both sexually and intellectually. And she felt a wonderful sense of happiness and security; "it was like a 'coming home' feeling in my body," she told me.

Three months after Margot began this visualization, which she says she did sporadically and sometimes skeptically, she met the man of her inner movie. In describing the unlikely circumstances of their meeting, she says that it was utterly uncanny how closely he resembled the pictures she had formed in her mind's eye. She knew instantly that it was he the moment she set eyes on him.

The relationship was everything Margot had dared to want it to be: passionate, tender, exciting, loving. But built into it was its own demise. Her lover, in New York for a special three-month program, had a family and a very successful career 3,000 miles away, to which he ultimately would return. Margot had omitted to visualize him free to grow into a long-term relationship.

As a postscript, she used her movies-of-the-mind to find out why this had happened, and discovered a current in her that was frightened of a committed relationship. That well-buried feeling had created its own reality. She is now visualizing, and expects to manifest, a relationship of love and trust that has no loopholes.

Jimmy, a divorced engineer, told me about his similarly enlightening experience using visualization to attract the woman he wanted to be with. He saw her as tall, striking, sympathetic, but also with a mind of her own. Two months later he found her. But after the initial attraction and passion he found the relationship missing an essential ingredient. He had omitted to put feelings of love into his pictures. And so he found his ideal woman, but he was unable to really give over to loving her.

"My consciousness wasn't expanded enough to see the whole picture when I was visualizing," he told me. He added that the "message" for him in this experience was that he needed to see what was blocking him from loving the woman of his dreams.

Anna, a vibrant and attractive professional in her fifties who had been divorced for a number of years, spent many months visualizing the kind of man she wanted to be with. She told me that she was very specific, and her expectations were very high. Among them was her hope that he would be a successful professional in a field related to her own, and that they would not only love together but also work together. She shared this story with me during their recent fifth wedding anniversary celebration. She told me that Charles, her husband and colleague, was everything she had visualized. Having observed them together for several years, I can tell you that theirs is, indeed, a very special relationship: loving, compatible, and deeply committed to their growth together.

How the Yoga of Sex Uses Visualization

Tantra Yoga, which is the philosophy of sex lifted from a biological function to a sacramental ritual, uses visualization in several different ways. I have always been very moved by Tantra, and especially by the implicit commitment to love and to experience another person totally in a spirit of joy and responsibility.

Visualization is used in contemporary Tantra to help potential lovers to attract each other, and then to enhance and deepen their contact.

In *New Age Tantra Yoga,* Howard John Zitko describes the process this way. "One mate must conceive in consciousness the characteristics that he wishes to have the other mate reflect. He must build up in his mind a well-defined image of what he expects the mate to be. Then he must call out on telepathic and intuitional levels for the response he anticipates. He must pour out his soul to his beloved, knowing that there is out there somewhere a soul whose need is comparable to his own and who has the same longing."

In the course of practicing the Tantra ritual, the couple use visualization by seeing each other in the nude and then closing their eyes "with the vision of their beloved as a being of light vibrating against a violet screen. They will train their minds to hold this picture of the other indefinitely, seeing the body suffused with light, surrounded by a halo of light, and projecting light beyond the immediate environment in which they are meditating. This creates an image within the consciousness of the partner which remains with the partner at all times. Thus they are never alone. One is within the other. . . ." From this practice the Tantra couple develop in addition to a very deep love and passion, a strong telepathic connection.

Other writings on Tantra tell how visualization can be used to keep the sexual feelings alive when a couple is making love. One of the ways this is done is to see with the inner eye energy flowing between the lovers and enveloping the merged sexual organs.)

Some Success Stories—and Their Scenarios

Your programmed visualizations are only as limited as your imagination—and your desires for yourself. Here, for inspiration, are some movie-of-the-mind experiences that have been shared with me.

Elizabeth had always felt that she could relate wonderfully to a man sexually *or* with feelings of love, but had rarely experienced both together. Her visualization focused on seeing energy stream between her heart and her pelvis. At the feeling level she experienced her longing to connect these two parts of herself. Her visualization has now become a reality for her. She told me that she regards her current happiness as a "semi-miracle!"

Peter created a visualization in which he saw his heart opening so that he could experience deep love. He saw it as a rose that he nurtured as he would a very rare and special flower, and in his imagery he watched it grow from a delicate bud to a full and mature flower. I should note that when I first met Peter he was a twice-married, very successful (materially), rather "macho" kind of man. There's now a gentleness about him that I had never seen before as he gets ready to marry again. This is the first time, he told me, that he will be marrying for love.

Jane, who's rather shy, had difficulty letting someone she meets for a first time know that she's interested in him or her. Now when she returns home, she told me, she sees the two of them on her screen having a good time together. "It's incredible, but within a couple of days I'll invariably meet that person on the street."

A young salesman I met while researching this book told me that he had used visualization to deal with a very difficult boss. Every morning he would see himself and his employer in a friendly situation where they were able to talk together with ease. On both the inner and outer levels he found himself increasingly liking this man he had so strongly disliked. His work situation changed so dramatically that his co-workers teased him about putting love potions in the boss's morning coffee!

A teacher shared with me that before she goes into her classroom she visualizes her students being stimulated, excited, and energized by the teaching experience, and having confidence in her as a teacher. It has had a very positive effect both on how she feels about her own abilities and how the class responds to her.

And one of my favorite stories comes from an elderly, very gentlemanly acquaintance of mine. "Whenever I see my wife feeling low," he told me, "I picture her being happy. Sometimes I see her doing something she loves to do—dancing, perhaps, or being with her grandchildren. I recall a time last year when she had been very depressed and we were on the street walking together. Out of the blue she took a few dance steps. It startled both of us, but it changed her whole mood!"

To Thine Own Self Be Loving

The absolutely most effective way to create excellent relationships, of course, is for *you* to feel whole and together and open to the rhythm of giving and receiving, which is what a relationship is all about. In this age of self-help, similar words have been said many times over, but I think they need to be repeated often. We all want the "magic" to come from *outside* ourselves and we yield so slowly to the reality that it can only come from *within* ourselves.

The truth is: *only when we feel our own self-worth, when we know and accept ourselves, when we allow ourselves to be happy, can we truly experience acceptance, fulfillment, and happiness with another person.*

That doesn't mean, of course, that we have to shelve our hopes for a meaningful relationship until we reach that ideal place within ourselves. But, hopefully, it does mean that seeking this state will continue to be a major focus in our lives. As the seeds which contain these parts of ourselves begin to flower, so will the relationships we create for ourselves.

Scripts for Relationships

This is a beautiful part of your process to bring your inner movies to—perhaps the most beautiful of all. As in other situations, the best visualizations are those that evolve spontaneously from within you. Here are some suggestions to get you started.

To Attract a Friend or Lover

See yourself as you want to be. Sense yourself as full, happy, and spilling over with light, love, and joy.

Visualize yourself as you want to be in a relationship. Actually create the *you* who reaches out to another in friendship or love. Feel what it feels like.

Where you sense yourself holding back, explore your resistance. See how you can change it.

See that you can be both strong and yielding in a relationship.

See that you can be the person you want to be *and* have the kind of relationship you want; it needn't be one *or* the other.

Shower yourself with white light to help you become whole.

Feel your longing to love and be loved.

Bring all your inner senses to this act of creating. Know that it is one of the most valuable gifts you can give yourself.

To Help You Through Your Most Negative Feelings

Ruth Carter Stapleton, a very lovely and serene woman for whom I have great respect, shared the following visualization for moving through deep feelings of anger or hatred. She calls it faith-imagination therapy.

When you find yourself utterly filled with rage or hatred, or both, over a situation in your life, allow yourself to relax and then relive the situation in its every detail in your mind's eye.

Take with you into the situation this time your adviser, or a figure that you know to be your guiding spirit, or a great spiritual person such as Jesus.

Be aware of this guiding spirit and let it be with you as the feelings come up and as you want to vent them on the person toward whom you feel them.

By doing this, you will find yourself released from that fury or hatred. Simply recreating the event with your positive intention to free yourself from it will have a very healing effect.

For Problems in Your Closest Relationships

Let the person with whom you are having difficulty appear on your screen. First, just see the face. Scan it very slowly, looking at the eyes, the eyebrows, the set of the chin, looking for frowns and lines which may indicate worry or anger. Let yourself stop at any point to really look at a part of the face you never really saw when you were together.

Now let that person's voice come into your movie. What are the first words that person says? What does he or she say to you that you have not been hearing?

Once the statement has been made, take three deep breaths before you answer. Simply be with the words you heard and digest them.

Now respond from your innermost being, not from those old words at the top of your consciousness.

Go back to observing your loved one with whom you are having problems, and take a new look at his or her face. See the effect your words have had. Simply let whatever happens be there.

Is there anything else he or she wants to say or do? Is there anything else you want to say or do? Let it happen.

Spend another moment being together, in the way you most want to be with each other. Remember the feelings you have for this person when there aren't problems between you.

To "Throw Light" on a Conflict with Someone You Love

The next time you and the special person in your life begin to argue heatedly, and you both feel that neither one understands the other, stop for a few moments and try this:

Face each other, hold hands, and with your eyes closed do a relaxation exercise together, perhaps one in which you focus on your breathing.

Now see white light radiating from the top of your head to the top of the other person's head and cascading down through his or her body. See white light then flow back to you from the other person.

When you feel filled with the other person's light, picture a blank screen on which you see the problem that has come between you. Now, wiping the problem off the screen, see the solution.

After a few moments of silence together, share what each of you have seen on your respective screens.

For Trouble in a Work Relationship

If you have been having problems with someone you work with (your boss, a co-worker, or someone on your staff) for either real or imagined wrongs, try this:

Imagine yourself in a very friendly situation where you and the other person are talking it all over, with each of you giving the other your feelings about the problem situation.

Picture yourself in that person's office or in yours. If you would feel more comfortable in a neutral setting such as a restaurant or bar, picture yourselves there.

Communicate to him or her, without anger, everything you truly feel about yourself, about the job you are doing, and about that person. Communicate in a way you have never let yourself do in real life.

Practice this every morning before you go to work. When you greet him or her in the office, note carefully what is real about the situation causing your upset and what you have added to it with your thoughts.

To Help You Complete a Separation

When a couple separates, it is often very hard to cut the emotional ties. This particular exercise may need to be repeated often.

See yourself tied with threads all over your body, and then see yourself tied to that other person you are no longer connected to in your actual life.

Now picture those threads unraveling and see them simply disappearing into the air. See the threads that were binding you simply float away. See yourself getting up, feeling free and happy, and moving away from the other person.

See yourself now on a path that leads toward light. See this path in front of you being as lovely and inviting as you can have it be.

Know that every ending is a new beginning. You can complete this experience. And you can also create a new experience that will be as loving and fulfilling as you want it to be.

11

Everything You Ever Needed to Know to Solve Your Problems

> When you accept that you are responsible for your life, you find out you just didn't happen to be lying there on the tracks when the train passed through. You are the asshole who put yourself there.
>
> —Werner Erhard

Most of us see ourselves as the victims of our problems. Our problems run *us*, rather than the other way around. We also believe that most of them—if not all of them—are caused or aggravated by circumstances beyond our control.

The truth is: all our problems have solutions, and these solutions reside within us.

Within each of us there is a place where we truly know the answer to any question or dilemma that we want to resolve. This part of us is often well-hidden, but it is not inaccessible.

The most important things ever said to us are said by our inner selves.

Visualization is a way to tune into this part of ourselves. As such, it is the most valuable and reliable way to discover whatever it is that we need to know—from finding a lost house key to finding a lost part of our psyche. Once we've found the solution to our problem then we can help ourselves put it to use through programmed visualization.

Many of you may not really know what the problems are

that run your life. You may not even believe that you have problems. But you experience a wanderlust, or an undefined malaise, or a vague dissatisfaction with the way things are. And a succession of negative things—some seemingly insignificant, some critical—seem to "just happen" to you. But nothing "just happens" to any of us. We are all fully responsible for our lives, and are the cause of each and every event in them. It is only because so many of us have a limited awareness of ourselves that we can't connect cause and effect, negative expectations with negative occurrences, our deepest needs with their realization. When we begin to make these connections, we then begin to transform our lives.

Getting Yourself Out of the Box You're In

A movie-of-the-mind script which I've used to help people discover what's wrong in their lives and how they can begin to change it involves the image of a closed box. I begin by having a person picture himself locked up in a giant wooden box with the lid securely fastened. "What would you do," I then ask, "to get out of your box?"

I did this recently in a series of business workshops designed to improve people's abilities to run their businesses creatively and profitably. In it, forty men and ten women used the movies of their minds to climb into their self-created boxes and then figure out how to get themselves out again. I want to point out that these were very successful people. When the idea was first presented to them they thought I was crazy and were convinced they couldn't do it; but when the picture-making process was over, every last one of them, with a childlike eagerness, wanted to share what he or she had seen.

A tall, lanky insurance executive confessed that at first he had felt frightened and claustrophobic. Then he had felt a surge of power and began to rock the box back and forth violently, "like a rowboat in a rough sea," and soon the box smashed open. He said that after he was thrown against the floor he righted himself and walked purposefully up to the company's president to tell him something he had wanted to say for a long time. "When I get back to the office," he announced happily, "I'm going to do just that."

A tense-looking man in the computer business said that he had just sat quietly in his box and contemplated his life. He was delighted to be where no one could reach him and felt a rare and welcome sense of peace. "I found that I need more time to myself," he shared. "I can't go on at the rate I'm going." As a result of this image he intended to find himself a place he would call "the box" where no one could find him.

A woman newly appointed mortgage officer in a bank had screamed for help in her box. "For the first time I realized that I really don't feel competent in my job. I'm always running to my new boss for help and feel afraid that I'm going to be found out." With that realization came another, that she really *was* competent to do the job.

Each person had seen a new dimension of self in this simple exercise. Not surprisingly, in later workshop sessions many would report changes they were making in their lives on the basis of what they had discovered in their inner movies.

No One Else Really Knows You

The use of visualization for problem-solving is one of the most remarkable aspects of this remarkable process. The biggest hurdle that stands between us and the solutions to our problems is that we don't fully trust that we can supply our own answers. Most of us would rather believe that someone else—a wise person, an infallible system, a very astute book, a therapist or guru or teacher—can tell us what in reality only we know. At best, other people can lovingly guide us back into ourselves. At worst, they can maintain the illusion that they are the bearers of our truth.

One of the reasons that we are the only ones who can solve our problems is that deep within ourselves we have stored up all the information that's related to the problem. Other people may know some of what we know, but nobody else can possibly duplicate all that we have experienced.

Another reason that we're our own best problem-solver is that we need to be able to merge what we know consciously with what we discover from our unconscious to transcend the two: the answer to the problem. In a deeply relaxed state, we also are receptive to a third element, and that is the greater intelligence, or universal mind, of which our own mind is but a part. These combined elements work more effectively than any other problem-solving approach I've experienced.

Liz: How Can I Get Unstuck?

Liz shared with me a series of inner movies that led, in two months, to dramatic changes in her life.

For some time she had been feeling reluctant to take the steps she knew were necessary to move forward in her life, to "take the plunge," as she described it. She felt stuck in a lot of areas, but most especially in her career. She gave the problem over to her inner process. The response that came was very clear: she needed to risk trusting her talents and abilities. She saw that, contrary to her belief, it was really very safe for her to move into a new career at this time. She was ready for this new phase in her life and simply needed to let herself give birth to it.

Then, as often happens, a programmed visualization was suggested. She needed to visualize, specifically, the life she wanted and try it on in her mind's eye. When she found a pattern and lifestyle that felt right, she was to visualize them regularly.

Liz began imagining a very specific daily schedule, which included work she wanted to do as well as a period every day when she would tune in to her inner source. She saw herself in her new career, which was doing life counseling, and interacting with those she would be working with. A former professional dancer who danced regularly with a group of friends, she imagined herself spending some time every day rehearsing and choreographing new work. She saw herself lunching with friends and spending time in the evening with her husband. And she observed herself moving through each day's activities looking happy. By mid-September, she told me with awe, her days were exactly as she had visualized them. She added that they were also exactly what she had wanted for a very long time.

Liz's experience is a possibility for all of us, although it may take a lot of time and practice—as was true in her case—before we can create this kind of deeply meaningful experience. I see all around me people who are ready to connect with this profound place in themselves. It is most obvious when, in visualization, they have the experience of having *known*, without quite knowing how they knew, that some decision or course of action is the right one as soon as they glimpse it on their inner movie screens.

Alice: How Can I Have Enough Money?

Alice shared with me a visualization in which the images that came up seemed so obvious and true that she laughed in recognition of them. It was clear to her that she had known for a long time what she saw inside herself that day, but had chosen not to know it consciously. (There are times when we are ready to face certain truths about ourselves, and there are other times when we're not, which is probably why certain material takes a long time to surface.)

The question posed to herself in this visualization was, "How can I let go of my anxiety about money, and trust that I can have enough as long as I'm willing to work and participate in the world?" Although in reality she always seemed to have enough money to meet her basic needs, and then some, she continued to worry that she wouldn't have enough for tomorrow, and the tomorrow after that one.

In her visualization she came upon a swimming pool. She made herself comfortable alongside it, with a cool drink in hand, and then noticed that her dearest friends were there as well. Suddenly, interrupting this idyllic scene, money began to rain down on them from the sky and fall into the pool. She then noticed that the money was wrapped in bales with metal strips around it and her friends were avoiding it. She looked at the bales carefully and saw that they were no longer money but had become fertilizer—"shit!" With this remarkable picture came words that told her that money would always rain down on her but that it was "shit," and as such meaningless. "All you have to do," she heard, "is to continue doing what you are doing. Worrying about money takes you away from giving to the moment, and *that* is what will bring the money to you."

Then the words guided her to what she needed to do. "The more you give to life, the more you will receive from it."

Pictures to Predict the Future

Using movies-of-the-mind for problem-solving can go far beyond solving personal problems. They can be used for problems relating to a business, a family, a community, even mankind-at-large. They are also quite remarkable used by groups for problems that concern the group.

One of the most fascinating uses of movies-of-the-mind occurs at the Center for the Study of Social Policy, a division of the Stanford Research Institute, where psychologists and scientists are visualizing to explore the future.

Dr. O. W. Markley, a social psychologist, describes himself as a "futurist." He is using visualization for what he calls "imagistic thinking," to look into the future so that we can begin to plan for it. Our logical, rational minds, he explained to me, are too abstract to create a holistic picture of what is to come. Through our intuitive minds, on the other hand, we can discover "what we already know."

When I visited with him at Stanford, rather than explain to me how he worked with this process, he offered to guide me through a visualization in which I would experience it myself. He suggested that I look at the problem of transportation, a subject he was currently researching. I demurred on the grounds that I had absolutely no knowledge or previous interest in transportation, but he was not to be dissuaded. He saw my naïveté as an advantage; my experience in other areas might throw new light on the subject.

"See yourself in Greece about 400 B.C.," he began. I closed my eyes and clearly saw myself in that place at that time. When I looked around at the people, it was uncanny to me how very real they were. I was especially aware of the way they were transported from place to place; they either walked or were riding in people-drawn carriages. At Dr. Markley's suggestion I then went on to early nineteenth-century New England, where, again, I saw myself interacting with (unfamiliar) friends and neighbors, and observed the styles of transportation. Moving into the present, I saw myself drive to an airport and board a plane; here, too, there were people and places that seemed very real but which I could not recall having experienced in my own life. In the final scene of this movie-of-the-mind, I projected myself into the year 2000. There I boarded an interesting-looking clear plastic bubble (unlike any-thing I recalled having seen in science-fiction films or books) and departed for another planet.

I was amazed at several things that happened in the visualiza-tion. The first was my very clear sense of how the style of transportation in any given period related to the lifestyle I observed; it affected not only the patterns of movement but also the entire way in which people lived and related to one another. The second surprise was the clarity of the details in the types and modes of transportation I observed. From this experience I understood how enormously valuable visualization could be for someone with advanced technical knowledge.

I left the Institute happily boggled by my experience and its implications for the future. Accompanying me was a formi-dable-looking report issued by the Center for the Study of Social Policy titled "Changing Images of Man," which turned out to be the most mind-boggling of my experiences that day. These visualizing scientists had concluded from their research that man in the future would live by "a self-realization ethic, placing the highest value on development of selfhood." Such a person, the report noted, would be "experimental, open-ended, and in touch with a divine self." They go on to say that "the basic nature of the universe is consciousness," that man is a manifestation of universal consciousness, and that *"all knowledge, power and awareness are ultimately accessible to man's consciousness."**

It was like the essence of Buck Rogers and Buckminster Fuller come together. A new age was really upon us.

Scripts for Problem-Solving

There are many effective visualization scripts that help us

---

* "Changing Images of Man, Policy Research Report 4," Center for the Study of Social Policy, Stanford Research Institute, 1974.

contact our inner place of knowing. The ones I most like to work with are included here. Others can be found in some of the books listed in the bibliography.

Guidelines Before You Begin

Look over the suggestions for creative insights in Chapter 9. The process is the same, and so the data applies equally to problem-solving.

Be aware of your attitude each time you consider visualizing for an answer to a question or problem.

1. Do you really want the answer?

2. Do you feel you really deserve it?

3. Are you willing to acknowledge whatever comes up, even if it is different from what you had hoped for, or is unflattering, or seems difficult to accomplish?

If your answer to any of these questions is *no,* then it might be best to focus first on your *resistance* to knowing the truth. How you can deal with your resistance could then be your first question.

Be aware that the answer might come in a different way or at a different time than you expect it. Quite often it comes in symbolic form, which you may need to translate.

Be conscious that you are waiting for an answer to a problem, and so be sensitive to the things that just seem to "pop" into your head, perhaps when you least expect them.

You might be tempted to go to the other extreme and never question what may come through. It is important for you to check out your answers against reality. You can also check them out by asking your inner consciousness further questions and dialoguing with it. This is not a static process. It is as alive as you are.

Finally, be aware that the problems in your outer life are

reflections of the problems in your inner life. And so your answer might not be the specific directions you might have hoped for. Instead, it may point to certain misconceptions about your life that you need to examine, or indicate situations that you have been avoiding and may now need to confront. Ultimately, this kind of direction from within is far more valuable than how-to-do-it advice—either from yourself or someone else.

Eye Tunnel*

Start by becoming deeply relaxed and going in your mind's eye to a very beautiful and peaceful place. Now think about the question you want to explore before you begin unreeling your inner movie and then put that question on your screen.

In this type of visualization it is helpful to have someone read the instructions to you, slowly, and allowing time for you to connect with the images. It is helpful for your guide to expand the directions to bring in all your senses—not only what you see, but also what you might hear, or smell, or feel tactually, and especially how you feel emotionally. It is not appropriate, however, for your guide to interpret your visualizations. Only you can and should do that.

Allow yourself to go deeper into relaxation until you discover a kind of hole, or even an eye, in your field of inner vision. Propel yourself toward that hole or eye./ You now see that it is really a tunnel./ On the other side of that tunnel is a place where you will discover what you are looking for./ Now go into that tunnel and go on through it quickly. Notice everything as you

* This is an abbreviated version of a script of the same name from Win Wenger. It was inspired by the common experience in Yoga meditation—and others as well—of seeing an eye in the inner vision. Win's scripts are fascinating and can be found in the book *Voyages of Discovery,* available by mail from Psychegenics Press, Box 332, Gaithersburg, Md., 20760.

go through, even fleeting impressions./ When you emerge you will find the solution to your problem, either directly or in some symbolic experience./ If you do not find it there immediately, follow the trail or path that you find there./ As you do, observe everything around you. The answer to your question is there./ Let yourself know it.

The theme of journeying in search of a great truth appears in myths of all cultures. Since these adventures are symbolic of the inner journey, they provide wonderful images for visualizations. And so, instead of going through an eye tunnel, at another time you might explore a long, winding path; or climb a steep mountain; or travel across the ocean to a beautiful foreign land. The answers you seek will be at the end of your journey.

The Control Room*

Allow yourself to go deeper into relaxation, and imagine an empty room that you are going to create into a master control room for your life.

First, picture a huge computer that can figure out any problem and decipher any code. At one end of the computer is a print-out or teletype machine. If you ask the computer a question, all you have to do is stand there and read the print-out for an answer.

Next, imagine a TV console with two picture screens on it. On the left-hand screen you can tune in to a woman guide who can answer any question you have. On the right-hand screen you can tune in to a male guide who can answer any question you have./   Now turn on the left-hand screen and see who your female guide is./   O.K., now turn that screen off and turn on

---

* This is adapted from a script used by Jack Canfield. est and other disciplines use similar visualizations.

the right hand screen and see who your male guide is./   O.K., now turn the right-hand screen off, too./   From now on any time you have a question about anything you can come into your special room, close the door, and using your computer or television screens, you can find out answers to help you./   Now ask your question and let the answer come.

Mirror of the Mind*

After you have clearly defined your problem, as honestly as you can, place the image of your problem within a blue frame./ Now pretend you are telling your problem to a friend. What would you be saying if the problem were solved? Be joyous in your voice and experience joy in your body./   Tell the friend what is happening. Tell them what your joy is like. Be specific./ Tell yourself, "I deserve the solution to my problem."/   See the solution in a white frame./   Tell yourself, "I will sense what is right for my highest good."/   Feel confident that the problem will be solved. There is no failure. There is only delayed success.

The Yellow Balloon**

Sometimes, rather than *solve* a problem, we need simply to *let it go.* This script might be especially appropriate for you if you feel that fear and guilt run your life.

Close your eyes and think of a container. Any kind you like will do: a plastic bag, a wastebasket, whatever comes onto your screen./   Into that container put all the things you can think of which you feel guilty about, which you are fearful about, which have been a painful experience for you./   Now imagine a large yellow balloon being filled with helium gas and then attached

---

* This is borrowed from the variation on a Mind Control script developed by Peggy Huddleston, director of the Philadelphia Mind Control Center.
** This is an adaptation of a script used by Dr. Gerald Jampolsky.

to your container./   Part of you wants to hang on to your container a while longer, but you decide to let it go./   As soon as you let it go, it goes up into the air. You can see the yellow balloon getting smaller and smaller, until it finally disappears./ Now notice how much lighter you feel./   Open your eyes and enjoy your new freedom.

12

The Mind Can Do Anything

We are all inseparable, interacting, ever-moving components of the universe.

—Dr. Fritjof Capra,
reporting on the new physics

As I walk along the street these days, I am often tempted to go over to someone who looks dazed, or is stumbling along "in a fog," and say to that person: "Wake up. Wake up to your own aliveness. Life is too precious to drag yourself through it unconsciously."

The more you use the movies-of-your-mind, the more you will find yourself waking up.

You will notice the difference in little things: your senses will be keener, and your delight in the everyday moments of your life far greater.

Then you will notice the difference as a whole new way of feeling about yourself and others. As you accept that you're responsible for your life, you stop feeling like a victim. As you stop feeling like a victim, you begin to take charge of your health and relationships and day-to-day problems. And as you begin to see what happens to you as *your* creation, you begin to create a life that is everything you want it to be.

You have discovered the incredible power of your mind. You have found that you can *know* and *become* far more than you ever dreamed possible. You have found that the whole you is greater than the sum of its parts—your intellect, your feelings, your body, your memories—and that you are connected to forces beyond yourself. And you have uncovered the exquisite jewel in you that is there to bring light into your darkness, and to continually guide and heal you.

Life is no longer just a chance series of frustrations, crises, and despair. Life now presents infinite possibilities and choices. Among them are all the joy and love and deep satisfaction that you deserve.

But the process doesn't end here. In one sense, it is only now beginning. The more alive and whole you become, the greater is your potential contribution in the world.

I see each of us as a link in a chain. We receive and we give. We take from one link and we pass on to the next. We are part of a continuing flow that moves through us and is affected by us.

This chain that we are each a part of is *the chain of happiness*. As links in it, the more each of us gives to ourselves and the more we become, the more we have that we can pass on to others. Since we cannot give something we do not have, we can serve as a link to happiness only by first being happy ourselves.

Visualization is itself a link in this chain by helping you to discover how you can create your own happiness. By using the techniques in this book to get to know the place where love, wisdom, and creativity reside within you, you give yourself a skill that takes you beyond yourself, to resonate throughout the universe.

This is the frontier of the New Age of Man. This is where we've arrived after 300 years of rejecting the inner self in the service of the "progress" of more comforts and greater conquests to satisfy the outer self.

Now we begin to see that the greatest adventure of all is the quest for self-knowledge. It is in piercing the mystery of who we are that we can experience oneness with all of life. Therein lies the long-promised heaven on earth.

I would like to leave you with one of the loveliest visualizations of all. You will find picturing these images a source of strength, peacefulness, healing, and renewal. When you direct this movie-of-the-mind, you bring the light of the universe into you and, with it, a powerful energy for when you need it most.

The Light of the Universe

Breathe deeply from your abdomen and feel yourself becoming wonderfully relaxed.

When you feel very deeply relaxed, begin to imagine yourself surrounded on all sides by golden light. Imagine a waterfall of this golden light a few inches above your head. Then begin to feel it flowing into the top of your head.

As it flows into you, feel its golden light pour through you, into your face and neck . . . into your arms and chest . . . into your heart . . . pouring down through your stomach and legs and feet until your whole body becomes part of the waterfall of golden light.

Bathe in this light. Feel it cascading through every part of you. Feel it flow from the top of your head, down through your body, and into the ground.

Feel yourself become one with this beautiful cascading golden light. Feel it a part of you, and you a part of it.

Know that in experiencing this golden light pouring into you, you allow the loving, healing forces of the universe into you, to help you.

Feel the beauty and the peacefulness and the health that is in you, and know that at all times you can be at one with yourself and the universe.

Bibliography

Ahsen, Akhter, *Psycheye.* New York: Brandon House, 1977.
    Explanation of Ahsen's particular imagery techniques as a therapeutic
    tool.
Assagioli, Roberto, *Psychosynthesis.* New York: Viking Press (Compass),
    1971.
Bach, Richard, *Illusions: The Adventures of a Reluctant Messiah.* New York:
    Delacorte Press, 1977.
    A delightful novel in which, among other things, the Reluctant Messiah
    teaches his friend how to visualize.
Benson, Herbert, *The Relaxation Response,* New York: Avon, 1976.
Bentov, Itzhak, *Stalking The Wild Pendulum: On the Mechanics of
    Consciousness.* New York: E. P. Dutton, 1977.
Birkinshaw, Elsye, *Think Slim—Be Slim.* Santa Barbara, California: Wood-
    bridge Press, 1976.
Bresler, David E., *What Is Pain?* and *Why Doesn't It Go Away?* Tapes.
    UCLA Pain Clinic, University of California at Los Angeles, Calif. 90024.
Brown, Barbara, *New Mind, New Body: Biofeedback: New Directions of the
    Mind.* New York: Harper & Row, 1974.
Bry, Adelaide, *est: 60 Hours That Transform Your Life.* New York: Harper
    & Row, 1976.
Capra, Fritjof, *The Tao of Physics.* Berkeley: Shambhala Publications, Inc.,
    1975.
    How Eastern thought and Western physics are related. Fascinating.
Castaneda, Carlos.
    All his books, which contain American Indian methods of teaching,
    use visualizations.
De Mille, Richard. *Put Your Mother on the Ceiling: Children's Imagination
    Games.* New York: Viking Press (Compass), 1973.
    Wonderful things to do with your children.

Friedman, Meyer, and Ray H. Rosenman, *Type A Behavior and Your Heart:* New York: Fawcett World, 1976.

Gallwey, W. Timothy, *The Inner Game of Tennis.* New York: Random House, 1974.

Ghiselin, Brewster, ed., *The Creative Process.* New York: New American Library, 1952.

Hendricks, Gay, and Russel Wills, *The Centering Book.* Englewood Cliffs, New Jersey: Prentice-Hall, 1975.

> Activities for children, parents, and teachers.

Huxley, Aldous, *The Art of Seeing,* New York: Harper & Row, 1942.

Jacobson, Edmund, *Progressive Relaxation,* Chicago: University of Chicago Press, 1942.

> This is the classic approach to the subject of relaxation, and forms the basis of most of the commonly used techniques today.

Journal of Mental Imagery. Bronx, New York: Brandon House, Inc., P.O. Box 240.

> This is a new biannual publication with an editorial board including many of those doing research in this field.

Jung, C. G., *Man and His Symbols.* Garden City, New York: Doubleday, 1968.

———, *Memories, Dreams, Reflections.* New York: Vintage Books, 1963.

> One of my favorite books.

LeShan, Lawrence, *The Medium, The Mystic and the Physicist.* New York: Ballantine Books, 1975.

Lewis, Howard R., and Martha E. Lewis, *Psychosomatics.* New York: Pinnacle Books, 1975.

Luthe, Wolfgang, *Autogenic Therapy.* New York: Grune & Stratton, 1969.

> An excellent relaxation and visualization system that is used extensively in the medical profession here and abroad.

Maltz, Maxwell, *Psycho-Cybernetics.* New York: Pocket Books, 1966.

> This has been a popular "bible" of visualizations. It tells wonderful success stories.

Masters, Robert, and Jean Houston, *Mind Games.* New York: Dell, 1972.

McKim, Robert, *Experiences in Visual Thinking.* Monterey, California: Brooks/Cole Publishing Co., 1972.

> A superb book, both great to look at and to read.

Murphy, Joseph, *Your Infinite Power to Be Rich.* West Nyack, New York: Parker Publishing Co., 1966.

> Using the technique for money.

Murphy, Michael, *Golf in the Kingdom.* New York: Dell, 1973.

Naranjo, Claudio, and Robert Ornstein. *On the Psychology of Meditation.* New York: Viking Press, 1971.

Ornstein, Robert E., *The Psychology Of Consciousness.* New York: Harcourt Brace Jovanovich, 1972.
Scholarly and worth reading.

Oyle, Irving, *The Healing Mind.* New York: Pocket Books, 1976.

———, *Time, Space and the Mind.* Millbrae, California: Celestial Arts, 1976.
Interesting account of how the mind can work if you'll let it.

Pelletier, Kenneth R., *Mind As Healer, Mind As Slayer.* New York: Delacorte Press, 1977.

Roberts, Jane, *The Nature of Personal Reality: A Seth Book.* Englewood Cliffs, New Jersey: Prentice-Hall, 1974.
This material, dictated in trance, discusses visualization extensively.

Samuels, Mike, and Hal Z. Bennett, *Be Well.* New York and Berkeley: Random House-Bookworks, 1974.

Samuels, Mike, and Nancy Samuels, *Seeing with the Mind's Eye.* New York and Berkeley: Random House, Bookworks, 1975.
This is far and away the best general book on the subject. It explores the history of visualization over 2,000 years as well as concepts and techniques. It's an excellent source book for those who seek to understand the subject in a larger context.

Schultz, J. H., and Wolfgang Luthe, *Autogenic Training: A Psychophysiological Approach to Psychotherapy.* New York: Gruen and Stratton, 1959.
Scholarly approach to the subject. Used as a basic reference.

Simonton, O. Carl, and Stephanie Matthews-Simonton, "Belief Systems and Management of the Emotional Aspects of Malignancy." *Journal of Transpersonal Psychology* 7, no. 1 (1975).

———, *Getting Well Again.* New York: J. P. Tarcher, 1978.
A self-help guide to overcoming cancer for patients and their families.

———, *Psychological Factors, Stress, and Cancer.* Cognetics, Inc., P.O. Box 592, Saratoga, Calif. 95070.
A collection of six tapes that include descriptions of the Simontons' work and their relaxation exercises and visualizations for cancer patients.

Singer, Jerome L., *Imagery and Daydream Methods in Psychotherapy and Behavior Modification.* New York: Academic Press, 1974.
A very scholarly book on the subject.

Smith, Adam, *Powers of Mind.* New York: Random House, 1975.

Spino, Mike, *Beyond Jogging: The Inner Spaces of Running.* Millbrae, Calif.: Celestial Arts, 1976.

Small and good paperback on the esoteric aspects of jogging.

Tart, Charles, ed., *Altered States of Consciousness.* Garden City, New York: Doubleday, 1969.

Toben, Bob, Jack Sarfatti, and Fred Wolf, *Space-Time and Beyond.* New York: E. P. Dutton, 1975.

A picture story which reduces complicated concepts about the physical universe to understandable terms.

Wenger, Win, *Noise-Removal Breathing; Energy Breathing and Starseed.* Tapes. Psychegenics Institute, Box 332, Gaithersburg, Md. 20760.

————, *Quick Work-Break, Relax/Recharge and General Meditative Relaxation; Question/Answer Adviser.* Tapes. Psychegenics Institute, Box 332, Gaithersburg, Md. 20760.

These are tapes which you can play for relaxing and other specific effects.

————, *Voyages of Discovery.* Gaithersburg, Md.: Psychegenics Press, 1977.

Win has many paperbacks available through his Psychegenics Institute. Good "how to" material.

Yogananda, Paramahansa, *The Autobiography of a Yogi.* Los Angeles: Self-Realization Fellowship, 1973.

Zitko, Howard John, *New Age Tantra Yoga.* Tucson, Arizona: World University Press, 1975.

Cassette Tapes on Visualization

Adelaide Bry has prepared tapes that, when used in conjunction with this book, will help you relax, get what you want, reduce stress. Two cassette tapes in book binder, shipping included, $29.95. Send money order to:

Adelaide Bry
P.O. Box 99088
San Diego, CA 92109

Index of Movie-of-the-Mind Scripts

General Index